PLANET
EARTH

THE FINAL CHAPTER

PLANET EARTH

THE FINAL CHAPTER

HAL LINDSEY

WESTERN FRONT

PLANET EARTH: THE FINAL CHAPTER

ISBN 1-888848-25-1

Published by WESTERN FRONT LTD., Beverly Hills, CA

Cover and interior design by Koechel Peterson & Associates, Minneapolis, Minnesota

Manufactured in the United States of America

CONTENTS

STAGE 4

More Beasts Than a Zoo
Oh, and the Other Kind of Beast
The Beast from the Sea
By the Numbers
Beast from the Earth
The Third Member of the Unholy Trinity
The First Seal
Peace, Peace, When There Is No Peace
Backed the Wrong Horse
Arafat—The Nobel Peacemaker
An "Inferior Peace"
The Koreish Treaty
Enter the Antichrist
A Relative Lull in the Action

SETTING
THE STAGE

SETTING THE STAGE

There have been a lot of books

published recently dealing with

the world situation, Bible prophecy,

and the time in which we live.

Most are confusing, or rely on subjective interpretation of the Bible, or follow no particular theological discipline. The purpose of this book is to arrange, in a chronological order, the following near-future developments—relying on the clear teaching of the Bible together with documented, developing trends in the global economy, the move toward a global government, and the growing movement toward a one–world religion. In this book, we will examine the following:

- The prophetic/historic events that lead up to the Tribulation's prelude
- The major events that will occur during the Tribulation
- The events of the Second Coming of Jesus Christ
- The events that set up the Millennial Kingdom

In the course of this examination, we will look closely at exactly what the Bible has to say concerning the Rapture of the Church. We'll look at the evidence for a Dispensationalist world–view as a necessary element of understanding Bible prophecy. We'll deal with the importance of Israel as the focal point of God's plan for the ages. As we progress, it will become clear how current events are rapidly moving us toward the fulfillment of that plan. There are a number of discernible stages, each of which relies upon the preceding, to form a kind of an interlocking puzzle in which each piece makes the Big Picture grow clearer.

We are well on the way, as I believe you will see, to the fulfillment of all the prophetic events connected with the Second Coming of Jesus, the Messiah. Jesus Himself foretold that the generation who saw the scenario of predicted signs begin to all fit together would be the one that would see them all fulfilled. There is little doubt, as you will see in the course of this book, that we are indeed living in that generation. I am more convinced than ever that we are the generation of which Jesus Christ spoke when He said, **"When these things begin to take place, straighten up and lift up your heads, because your redemption is drawing near"** (Luke 21:28).

CHAPTER 1

THE MOST UNLIKELY NATION ON EARTH

"Therefore prophesy, and say to them,
'Thus says the Lord GOD, "Behold, I will
open your graves and cause you to come
up out of your graves, My people; and
I will bring you into the land of Israel." '

"Therefore, say to the house of Israel,...
'It is not for your sake, O house of Israel,
that I am about to act, but for My holy
name, which you have profaned among
the nations where you went.' " [1]

---

[1] Ezekiel 37:12; 36:22.

The most certain proof that we are living out the final chapter of human history can be found in the existence of a tiny country in the Middle East. The entire nation is about the size of Connecticut. Its capital city is so small (population 500,000) that it should scarcely rate mention among the great cities of the region—let alone the planet.

Its people have been victims of hatred almost everywhere they have fled for refuge for nearly 2,000 years. They have continually been the subjects of pogroms and genocide campaigns. That the Jew has continued to exist as a distinct race, in view of the horrible circumstances in which he continually lived, defies natural explanation.

Yet today, Israel is. The people who against all odds remained a distinct nation in exile has returned to its ancient homeland and been reborn as a nation.

Israel continues to stand, having been victorious five times over the combined might of the Muslim armies. Its defense force is one of the best in the world in spite of countless UN resolutions that appear aimed at weakening Israel's ability to defend itself against its enemies. Israel's economy prospers despite total regional boycotts aimed at destroying its economy.

We'll examine the various elements that make Israel a miracle country and the preamble to man's final chapter, but first, we'll put together a sort of "overview" of the history of this, the most unlikely ethnic nation on the face of Planet Earth.

THE BEGINNING OF ISRAEL'S WOES

Israel was conquered and destroyed by King Nebuchadnezzar of Babylon for the first time in 606 BC. Jerusalem was laid waste, and the people of Israel were taken captive—many of them were transported to Babylon as slaves. Beginning in 536 BC, the Jews were allowed to return to Judea, to rebuild Jerusalem, and live in the land, but they were never again sovereign. Israel existed as a province in a succession of empires: Babylon, Media–Persia, Greece and, finally, Rome.

During this period, they dwelt in the land, but did not possess it in the sense of having an independent government. They lived as a people under occupation until AD 70, when the Roman legion under Titus was dispatched to Jerusalem to put down the latest in an endless series of rebellions. But the Romans finally said "enough" and sought to destroy Israel as a nation and distinct people. According to the Jewish contemporary historian, Flavius Josephus, more than a million Jews were slaughtered, the Jewish Temple was utterly destroyed, and the surviving Jews were scattered as slaves.[2] Jews were forbidden to assemble into groups of more than three under pain

---

[2] Josephus, an eyewitness to the events, wrote, "While the Temple was in flames, the victors stole everything they could lay their hands on, and slaughtered all who were caught. No pity was shown to age or rank, old men or children, the laity or priests—all were massacred. As the flames roared up, and since the Temple stood on a hill, it seemed as if the whole city were ablaze. The ground was hidden by corpses, and the soldiers had to climb over heaps of bodies in the pursuit of fugitives" (Josephus, *The Essential Writings*, translated by Paul L. Maier).

of death. Most ended up settling outside of Israel in ghettos on the European or Asian continents, where they remained—segregated and despised by their hosts—for two millennia.

Through these centuries, the descendants of Abraham, Isaac and Jacob endured one pogrom, persecution and vilification after another. Each generation suffered some new humiliation and suffering. Still the homeless, wandering Jew kept himself separate and hoped in the promises of his prophets. Against all odds, he remained a nation without a homeland. In hope against hope, he prayed at each Passover, "Next year in Jerusalem." This was an expression of his most fervent hope that kept him from total despair. But nothing could change the hapless Jew's lot until the time appointed by the Hebrew Prophets.

MOSES GAVE REASON FOR THE SECOND DISPERSION

"Do not think that I will accuse you before the Father; the one who accuses you is Moses, in whom you have set your hope. For if you believed Moses, you would believe Me; for he wrote of Me. But if you do not believe his writings, how will you believe My words?"[3] So Jesus of Nazareth warned the generation that would experience the Roman holocaust. For Moses had predicted the fate of the nation of Israel when it

[3] John 5:45–47 NASB.

would reject GOD's ultimate Prophet, "**And the
LORD said to me, 'They have spoken well. I will
raise up a prophet from among their country-
men like you, and I will put My words in his
mouth, and he shall speak to them all that I
command him. And it shall come about that
whoever will not listen to My words which He
shall speak in My name, I Myself will require it
of him.' "**[4]

Moses even predicted the horrible consequences of
Israel's rejection of His ultimate Prophet, the Messiah:

"**Moreover, the LORD will scatter you among all
peoples, from one end of the earth to the other
end of the earth; and there you shall serve other
gods, wood, stone, which you or fathers have
not known. And among those nations you shall
find no rest, and there shall be no resting place
for the sole of your foot; but there the LORD will
give you a trembling heart, failing of eyes, and
despair of soul. So your life shall hang in doubt
before you; and you shall be in dread night and
day, and shall have no assurance of your life. In
the morning you shall say 'Would that it were
evening!' And at evening you shall say, 'Would
that it were morning!' because of the dread of
your heart which you dread, and for the sight of
your eyes which you shall see. And the LORD will
bring you back to Egypt in ships, by the way
about which I spoke to you, 'You will never see**

---

[4] Deuteronomy 18:17–19 NASB.

it again!' And there you shall offer yourselves for sale to your enemies as male and female slaves, but there will be no buyer."[5]

This is a tragically accurate prophecy of Israel's second destruction and dispersion by the Romans in AD 70.

A PROPHECY OF HOPE IN A SEA OF DESPAIR

The Prophet Ezekiel recorded a startling prophecy in Ezekiel Chapter 37. It is usually described as the "vision of the dry bones." He saw a valley filled with the dry, disjointed bones of thousands of human skeletons lying in open graves. As he watched, the bones began to come together and grow flesh. Then the corpses came to life and stood up, **"an exceedingly great army"** (v 10).

As the prophet continued to stare in astonishment, the Lord unveiled the meaning of the vision. The Lord revealed to him that the disjointed, dry bones symbolized the whole house, or nation, of Israel and the horrible plight they would face while dispersed among the Gentiles. The graves represented the gentile nations into which they were forced to flee. The fact the graves were open portrayed that the gentile nations were not to be the permanent dwelling place of the Israelites. The coming together of the resurrected bones to form a great army is a prophetic picture of the magnitude of the miracle God swore He would perform in restoring the dispersed nation to its ancient homeland of Israel.

---

[5] Deuteronomy 28:64–68 NASB.

This graphic, prophetic allegory accurately describes the history of the nation and people in dispersal among the nations for two and a–half millennia. The Lord promised further that He would cause the nation of Israel to be reborn in the same land from which He scattered them. He said this would all take place in the days that would immediately precede the Messiah's coming as their Deliverer and King.

A TWO–KINGDOM RESURRECTION MIRACLE

It is very important to note that more than 250 years before the time of Ezekiel's vision, a civil war had taken place that divided the nation into two kingdoms. The Assyrians conquered the Ten Tribes of the Northern Kingdom, called Israel in 722 BC. This was the result of a long period of unbelief and apostasy. The Ten Northern Tribes were hopelessly dispersed among the nations by the time of Ezekiel.

It wasn't until 606 BC that God's patience became exhausted with Judah's unbelief. King Nebuchadnezzar of Babylon conquered the Southern Kingdom, known as Judah for the first time in 606 BC, exactly as God had forewarned through His Prophets. He left a token number of Jews there and had the rest carried off to Babylon as slaves. When the appointed king, Jeconiah, rebelled, Nebuchadnezzar returned in 586 BC and utterly destroyed Jerusalem and the Temple. All survivors were carried off as slaves.

Ezekiel was among this group of captives taken to Babylon. He wrote the Book of Ezekiel while in captivity. Keep in mind the fact the dispersion of the

Northern Kingdom of Israel was already history in Ezekiel's time. The Southern Kingdom of Judah was all that remained, and it was called Judah, not Israel. That is why the descendants of Isaac are today called Jews, rather than Israelites. It came from the name Judah. Even so, Ezekiel faithfully recorded the future restoration of the already long–dead northern nation of Israel together with Judah in the "last days"!

THE MIRACLE OF A NAME

In his book, *Personal Witness,* Ambassador Abba Eban, one of Israel's Founding Fathers and Israel's first Foreign Minister, wrote:

> "In accordance with our plan, a letter from [Chaim] Weizmann to [President] Truman had been sent on May 13 asking him to recognize our new state. The expected infant state was still nameless, since the Zionist leaders were still characteristically, arguing over the name (should it be 'Judea.' 'Zion,' what about the name 'Israel'?). Weizmann, for the first time in history, was asking for a nameless state to be recognized...."[6]

Although Ezekiel confidently wrote of the restored Jewish state as "Israel" 2,500 years before, those who actually served as midwives to the rebirth did not decide on the name until the very day before!

THE DREYFUS AFFAIR

In December 1894, a military court in closed session

---

[6] Abba Eban, "Personal Witness," p. 144, Putnam, © 1992.

found Captain Alfred Dreyfus, a Jew from Alsace, guilty of espionage on behalf of Germany. He was sentenced to life imprisonment on Devil's Island, a colony off the coast of French Guyana.

However, in 1896 evidence emerged that Major Eszterhazy was guilty of the crime and that Dreyfus had been wrongly accused. Georges Picquart, head of Military Intelligence, had uncovered this information but was ordered to remain silent. Picquart was then sent to Tunisia, but public opinion demanded an inquiry. Although Eszterhazy was arrested he was later acquitted.

In January 1898, Emile Zola, outraged by the turn of events, wrote his famous article, "J'accuse," in which he claimed that there had been a miscarriage of justice. With the publication of his article the mood in France escalated to fever pitch and the country was split between Dreyfusards and anti–Dreyfusards. Matters deteriorated when Picquart was court–martialed and sentenced to prison. Despite a review of his case, Dreyfus was again found guilty but his sentence was reduced to ten years. Shortly thereafter, President Emile Loubet pardoned Dreyfus, who accepted the verdict, although advised not to. In 1906, however, Dreyfus was fully exonerated and promoted to the rank of major.

While the Dreyfus case had strong anti–Semitic overtones, it was not this fact alone that made it such a cause célèbre. France was divided into two distinct camps at this time: clericalists vs. free thinkers, monarchists vs. republicans, reactionaries vs. liberals and militarists vs. skeptics. For Jews, the Dreyfus affair was a harsh reminder of the persistence of anti–Semitism.

This incident caused only a few Jews to embrace Zionism. Theodor Herzl himself had in all likelihood reached this conclusion before Picquart's revelations and certainly prior to Zola's article, "J'accuse." But this affair seemed to solidify Herzl's convictions that the Jews would never be safe apart from having their own homeland.

THE ZIONIST CONGRESS— WHEN "THE BONES FIRST RATTLED"

In 1897, Theodore Hertzl, a reporter who had covered the Dreyfus trial, came to the conclusion that the Jews would never be accepted in the gentile world, even if they sought to be loyal citizens as Dreyfus had. He was also convinced by the long tragic history of anti–Semitism that no place was ultimately safe for the Jew. He pleaded his case with the Jewish leaders of Europe about the need to find a homeland for the Jewish people. The idea became known as Zionism—named for Mount Zion in Jerusalem.

ZIONISM—AN IDEA WHOSE TIME HAD COME

Finally, a group of Jews caught Herzl's vision. They convened their first meeting in 1897 in the city of Basel, Switzerland, calling themselves Zionists. At that time, they were willing to accept whatever land they could get to establish a state. They even asked England to allow them to establish the Jewish homeland in the British colony of Uganda. England denied the request, suggesting to them that they should instead look toward their ancestral home of Palestine. Palestine was a neglected part of the Turkish Ottoman Empire with very few inhabitants at the time.

Encouraged by England's suggestion, they began to emigrate to the land of Palestine. Emigration to Palestine was slow at first. Many European Jews had become accustomed to the softer life and culture of the cities of Europe. The idea of settling in the harsh, forbidding desert wasteland of Palestine as pioneer farmers had little appeal to them. Those few hardy souls that were willing to go were widely viewed by more secular Jews as "religious zealots." Besides, at this point in history, European civilization was more tolerant of the Jews, mainly because of their contributions to art, literature, medicine and science. As long as they kept to the ghettos, European Jewry was relatively secure and wealthy. Ironically, of all the Jews in Europe, those who lived in Germany sought the hardest to assimilate and be accepted as Germans, not Jews.

Nevertheless, the mystical attraction of God's land to its ancient people became very strong, so a significant Jewish population settled there over the next few years. Supernaturally, the land began to respond to the returning exiles, just as God through Ezekiel had promised it would: **"Therefore prophesy concerning the land of Israel and say to the mountains and hills, to the ravines and valleys: 'This is** what the Sovereign Lord says: I speak in my jealous wrath because you have suffered the scorn of the nations. Therefore this is what the Sovereign Lord says: I swear with uplifted hand that the nations around you will also suffer scorn. But you, O mountains of Israel, will produce branches and fruit for my people Israel, for they will soon come home. I am concerned for you and will look on you with favor; you will be plowed and sown, and I will multiply the number of people upon you, even the whole house of Israel. The towns will be inhabited and the ruins rebuilt.' "[7]

A MIRACLE FROM SMOKELESS GUNPOWDER

During World War I, a British scientist, Dr. Chaim Weizmann, developed a synthetic acetone that helped the British to develop new, smokeless gunpowder, which significantly shortened the war. In gratitude, the British government offered to grant Weizmann a "boon." Weizmann, a Zionist leader, asked for a homeland for his people. His request resulted in the issuance of the Balfour Declaration, which said in part:

> "His Majesty's government view with favor the establishment in Palestine of a national home for the Jewish people, and will use their best endeavors to facilitate the achievement of this object...."

Lord Balfour had become an avid believer in the literal interpretation of Bible prophecy, through the influence

---

[7] Ezekiel 36:6–10 NIV.

of John Darby's extensive ministry. As a result, he believed that God could not lie to the Jewish people when He promised to return them to their own land and reestablish the State of Israel. Lord Balfour, with the assistance of another Member of Parliament named Lord Lindsay, who also believed in the literal promises of Bible prophecy, had exerted considerable influence on their colleagues for the sake of seeking to help establish a Jewish homeland.

PROVIDENCE BEGINS TO WORK

In December 1917, at the height of World War I, Britain found itself in a position to implement the Balfour Declaration. In the providence of God, General Allenby captured Palestine from the Ottoman Empire—ending 400 years of Turkish Muslim rule.

At the end of the war, the League of Nations dismantled the Ottoman Empire and divided the Middle East between two peoples, the Arabs and the Jews. Of the land apportioned to the Jews by the Balfour Declaration in 1917, only some 20% was actually given the Jews by 1921. The remainder of the promised Jewish homeland was awarded to the Arabs. This was due to an unexpected furor among the Muslims, who suddenly found the neglected and desolate land of Palestine to be of infinite value. (There will be more about this later in the book.)

A BRITISH POLICY THAT ENDED THE EMPIRE

The British immigration policy for Palestine underwent

several modifications during the years between the wars. As the Arabs objected to the influx of Jewish refugees fleeing Europe, Britain changed the rules to curtail Jewish immigration into Palestine. Britain's need for Arab oil became more important than keeping its promise to the Jews. In 1930, the White Paper was passed through Parliament, effectively banning further Jewish immigration to Palestine.

In March 1939, the British government actually asked the Germans to "discourage travel" by Jews to the Holy Land. According to official documents, Sir Neville Henderson sent the following cable to the Nazi Foreign Office.

> "There is a large irregular movement from Germany of Jewish refugees, who, as a rule, set out without visas or any arrangements for their reception, and they attempt to land in any territory that seems to them to present the slightest possibility of receiving them. This is a cause of great embarrassment to His Majesty's government, and as it appears, to the American government, and the latter have expressed a wish that you should join the American charge d'affaires in Berlin in bringing the situation to the attention of the appropriate German Authorities and requesting them to discourage such travel on German ships."[8]

Certain elements within the British Foreign Ministry became hostile toward the Jews, especially some of the personnel working in Palestine. Because of this attitude, many millions of Jews who might have

---

[8] Foreign Office to Sir Neville Henderson: Treasury Papers 188/226.

escaped the Nazis perished in their SS extermination camps.

This kind of action not only sealed the fate of the Jews, but of the British Empire. God warned the gentile world 4,000 years ago of what He would do to the people or nation who harmed His people simply for being Israelites. He promised Abraham, Isaac and Jacob concerning their descendants, **"I will bless those who bless you, and I will curse the one who curses you."**[9] The rise and fall of many great gentile empires of history can be traced to how they blessed or mistreated the Israelites.

After World War II, the Empire "on whose flag the sun never set" found itself being progressively destroyed. Today, the United Kingdom is only a shadow of what it was.

THE NAZI HOLOCAUST

The land of Israel continued to call out to the Jewish people, but immigration began to dwindle. Fewer and fewer were willing to trade the relative comfort of Europe for the brutal Judean wilderness. But conditions in Europe quickly deteriorated for the Jews. Adolf Hitler's Nazi Party started slowly—blaming the Jews for everything from the loss of World War I to the crippling war reparations demanded of Germany by the Treaty of Versailles.

Ultimately, Hitler took the persecution of the Jews to a new level. Instead of rounding them up, stealing

---

[9] Genesis 12:3

their property and placing them in ghettos as in times past, the Nazis decided to eliminate them all— men, women and children. The Nazis rounded up all the Jews they could find—starting in Germany, and repeating the process in each country they occupied. The Jews were crammed into cattle cars and transported to extermination camps like Auschwitz, Treblinka and Dachau.

They were led like sheep to the slaughter into gas chambers where they were murdered with cold efficiency. Their corpses were rendered for soap. Their skin was made into lampshades. Their women's hair was cut off and used to stuff mattresses. Their teeth were extracted for their gold fillings. Their bones were ground into meal for fertilizer. Finally, whatever was left was consigned to the ovens. Six million men, women and children marched naked to their deaths, resigned to their fate. The rabbis explained that this was simply the tradition of the Jewish people, the eternal victims.

THE "NEVER–AGAIN–COMPLEX" FACTOR!

The survivors emerged from the Nazis Holocaust a different people. When the full story of the Holocaust became public, nations were visibly shocked. But for some, the shock quickly wore off as the survivors were transformed in the public mind from "pitiable victims" into "problem refugees." Everything they owned—homes, property and bank accounts—had been confiscated before the war. The new owners agreed it was a shame, but did nothing to right the wrong. Greed proved once again to be a universal human weakness.

Before the Holocaust, the Jews were unwilling to trade what little they had in Europe for the material austerity and hard work of building a home in the Judean wilderness. But the war changed all that. The battered survivors of Hitler's madness found themselves with nowhere to go and no country willing to receive them. Suddenly, Zionism was more than a religious ideology. It was the only hope for a people to whom hope had always been a stranger.

MAY 14, 1948—THE COUNTDOWN BEGINS

The Jews of Europe became the Israelis of Palestine— tough, disciplined and courageous in the face of overwhelming odds. With their backs to the wall, no place to go and a firm conviction that the survival of the race was at stake, they learned to be formidable soldiers.

They fought against British immigration restrictions to sneak themselves into Palestine by any means. They fought against a hostile Muslim population that was being flooded with new Muslim residents from all over the Muslim world. When the British disarmed them and heavily armed the Muslims, they smuggled weapons in with incredible cunning and audacity.

They organized freedom fighting cell groups that gave the British more than they could handle. The British withdrew, and Israel claimed the land of Palestine to be the Jewish homeland on May 14,

1948. They proclaimed a new State and providentially named it ISRAEL.

The next day, they were invaded on all sides by the combined might of the Muslim world. Humanly speaking, there is no way to explain how the Israelis defeated the well–trained, heavily armed Muslim army that outnumbered them ten to one.

A MODERN MIRACLE

The restoration of Israel was a modern miracle in every sense of the world. Its continuing survival is an even greater miracle.

Never in history has such a thing happened. From being scattered across the face of the earth for two millennia, they returned to the same piece of real estate from which they were driven. They brought with them their culture, preserved through the centuries—their religious laws, their dietary laws, their customs. And in spite of 2,000 years of exile without a nation—usually living under horrible conditions that would have broken any person's spirit—they kept alive a sense of nationhood that somehow survived in their hearts.

The empires of the Assyrians and Babylonians of this world all rose and fell. Israel alone—scattered, without friend, land or flag—has endured to become a nation again. There are no Jebusite people in the world today, no Babylonians, no Medes, no Amalekites, no Caananites or Philistines. But Israel exists, as it did before Nebuchadnezzar!

ISRAEL'S NATIONAL LANGUAGE IS A MIRACLE

Fulfilling the words of the prophet Zephaniah, even the Hebrew tongue, a dead language even before the days of the Roman occupation, is the working language of Jerusalem today. Conversational and working Hebrew was restored by Jewish scholar Ben Yehuda in the early 20th century, but did not replace Yiddish until 1948. But all this was no accident—it had been foretold. Listen to the words of the 5th century BC Hebrew prophet, Zephaniah:

> **"For then I will give to the peoples purified lips, that all of them may call on the name of the Lord, to serve Him shoulder to shoulder.' "[10]**

Those of us who have lived through a major part of the 20th century have witnessed this miracle of prophetic fulfillment with our own eyes.

TICK...TICK...TICK...

When the six-pointed Star of David ascended for the first time over the Jewish ancestral homeland, the countdown to the end of the present age had begun. **"Now learn this parable from the fig tree: When its branch has already become tender and puts forth leaves, you know that summer is near. So you also, when you see all these things** [i.e., the predicted signs], **know that it is near—at the very doors. Assuredly, I say to you, this generation** [that sees the signs] **will by no means pass away till all these things are fulfilled. Heaven and earth will**

---

[10] Zephaniah 3:9 NASB.

pass away, but My words will by no means pass away."[11]

This fig tree parable we are commanded to learn is all about how to recognize a general time. Just as the first leaves on the fig tree mean that the general time of summer is near, so when the things predicted to immediately precede the return of Jesus Christ all begin to appear within the same time frame, we are to know we are living in the generation of His coming.

The rebirth of Israel was the key sign around which all of the other prophetic signs began to appear in concert with each other. Never before had this explicitly predicted unique scenario of events appeared in history. And this scenario is so constructed that once its events did fit into place, they could never be unscrambled and occur again. In other words, once the predicted events all appeared, they had to lead on to the final fulfillment in the Second Coming of Jesus Christ.

There can be no mistake about it, we are now living in the generation of "the fig tree." We are living in the generation that will witness the climactic fulfillment of prophecy—the Rapture of the Church followed by a global holocaust that will be ended by the visible return of Jesus Christ to earth.

Stay tuned. Much more is coming.

---

[11] Matthew 24:32–35 NKJV.

CHAPTER 2
THE PROPHETIC AWAKENING

An overlooked but extremely important

development of history that immediately

preceded the birth of Zionism was the

great awakening to literal interpretation

of Bible prophecy.

At the beginning of 19th century, theologians began to apply the same principles of literal interpretation to the field of prophecy that the Reformers had applied to the doctrines of Salvation. This caused a kind of "reawakening" to the reality of Bible prophecy and its growing relevance to the time in which they were living. After the close of the 1st century AD, there had developed apathy toward the study of prophecy. By the 4th century, prophecy had been written off as a collection of allegories. Such early theologians as Origin and Augustine allegorized prophecy into meaningless nonsense.

Around the middle of the 19th century, as we saw in the last chapter, the key to biblical prophecy about the Last Days began to stir. The descendants of Abraham, Isaac and Jacob began to migrate back to the land of Palestine in significant numbers.

This confirmed to men like John Nelson Darby that the literal interpretation of prophecy was the only correct interpretation. Darby had already concluded before the middle of the 19th century that Israel had to be literally reborn in its ancient homeland. So when the Zionist movement was formed, teachers in the new prophetic movement got excited.

Darby attended Trinity College of Dublin, Ireland, where a professor, Richard Graves, was an advocate for the Jewish people in the British Empire. Graves held a series of important prophecy conferences— the most famous of which were held in New York in 1878 and Chicago in 1886.

Graves was a Bible literalist who wrote a series of articles for *The Baptist* Magazine. In his articles, Graves wrote that since "the Jews' dispersion is literal, so will their restoration be literal." He also argued for a gentile "parenthetical period," or a gap period in which the unconditional promises to Israel are postponed, not annulled. He held that despite Israel's rejection of Jesus as Messiah, the Old Testament promises to Abraham and his seed concerning their homeland and nation were unconditional. Graves' theology probably had a profound affect on Darby.

Darby emphatically believed the Jews would return to Palestine and become a nation again. He also began to study just how long the spotlight of God's dealing would remain on the Gentiles. He argued that the current ascendancy of the Gentiles had to be a "parenthetical period" that by no means annulled God's unconditional promises to Israel. He taught that despite their rejection of Jesus as their Messiah, the Old Testament promises to Abraham and his seed concerning their homeland were irrevocable.

Most theologians from Augustine onward had declared the promises and blessings of Israel null and void and transferred them to the Church—without the curses, of course. Most anti–Semitism within the professing Christian church from that time onward was fueled by the belief that God was finished with the Jew as a special people and nation. Therefore, making life "difficult" for the Jew became almost a mark of religious dedication.

Darby began to study the different ways God dealt with people down through the ages. As his studies progressed, he found his views changed. By 1833, Darby had formulated the theological position called Premillennial Dispensationalism. Don't let these words freak you out.

PREMILLENNIAL DISPENSATIONAL WHAT??

The doctrine of premillennialism means that Jesus Christ must return at a time of global holocaust to rescue His people and then establish an earthly kingdom for them of 1,000 years' duration.

Dispensationalism is simply God's outline of history that divides it into several stages of history that are discernible by a careful, inductive study of the Bible.

The Bible recognizes the principle of dispensations when it speaks of **"ages past**," **"this present age"** and **"ages to come"** (see Ephesians). Dispensationalism recognizes that God spoke at different times, in different ways, to different ages of humanity, according to His plan for the successive stages of history.

Each dispensation ends with human failure under the conditions of that dispensation. There is then a Divine judgment that ends the old and a new revelation that initiates the new dispensation.

Each new dispensation is characterized by three things: first, an annulling of certain conditions of the old; second, a continuation of certain conditions; and third, a revelation of new promises and responsibilities.

The means by which a believer walks with God has changed in the various dispensations, in accordance with the divinely orchestrated progress of revealed truth about God.

There is one thing, however, that remains constant throughout all dispensations—salvation is always by grace through faith alone. God's character cannot change; therefore, the basis upon which He accepts a man must remain the same. That is, if man cannot earn God's acceptance by his good works today, then man could never at any time gain God's acceptance by works. For man's fallen nature remains the same and God's holiness is the same today, yesterday and forever—and never the twain shall meet!

In English, there are three main ideas connected with Dispensationalism. First, it's God's way of dealing out, or distributing, His plans and intentions for a particular segment of the human race under given circumstances at specific times.

Second, it's the action of administering, ordering or managing.

Third, it is the action of dispensing with some responsibilities for the recipients. The *Oxford English Dictionary* explains it as "a stage of progressive development, expressly adapted to the needs of a particular nation or group during a specific period of time."

It can also be *the age or period during which a Divinely instituted system has prevailed.* The Greek word *oikonomia,* (οἰκονομία) on the other hand, comes from a verb that means "to manage, regulate, administer and plan." The word itself is a compound of two words whose root meanings mean, simply, law of the house. They came to mean, literally, "to divide, apportion, administer or manage the affairs of an inhabited household."

The most essential things to remember about Dispensationalism are these: first, the Church is distinct from Israel in God's plan, and, secondly, God's overall purpose is to bring glory to Himself.

Darby's understanding of Dispensational truth not only opened the door to understanding end–time prophecy, but it also brought segments of the Church back into fellowship with the Jews. The concept of Church–sponsored anti–Semitism waned. Instead, the Church began to see the restoration of the Jews to their homeland as part of God's plan for the end of this present dispensation, and eagerly anticipated it.

Darby's theology had a great impact in America, and so it comes as no surprise that America was the first country in history to extend the right to vote to a Jew. In all other countries, Jews were Jews, regardless of where they were born. In the United States, a Jew is legally first an American, and his Jewishness is a matter of personal conscience.

BEGINNING OF UNDERSTANDING

At the beginning of the 20th century, Dispensationalism was one of the driving forces in the rise of evangelical Christianity and Fundamentalism. Multitudes were converted, and a great interest in Bible prophecy was kindled. Prophecy conferences and camp meetings began to spring up all across the United Kingdom and the United States. The central focus of those meetings was the prophecies concerning the regathering of Israel to the Land of Promise. By understanding the dispensations, prophecy teachers were able to distinguish that which had been fulfilled from that which was yet future. And, the overwhelming body of prophecy for the last days was directly related to a restored nation of Israel in the Land of Promise. Until that happened, nothing else could. But when the land was reunited with her people, the floodgates would open, and this present dispensation would draw to a close.

Unfortunately for the Jews, the view held by evangelicals is and remains a minority view among professing Christianity. Not everyone who believes Bible prophecy is a Dispensationalist—and not everyone who believes in Bible prophecy believes God has a purpose for the Jews. Understandably, to the average Jew there is little—if any—difference between a Catholic, a Mormon, a Jehovah's Witness, a Presbyterian, a Baptist or a Dispensationalist. To a Jew, they're all Christians, and the Cross remains the symbol of their persecution.

THE BEGINNING ROOTS

The modern movement for a Jewish homeland did not begin with the Holocaust. It actually grew out of a series of violent attacks, known as pogroms, leveled against the Russian Jews in the 1880s under the czars of Russia. In 1882, a group of Jewish exiles met in Constantinople. Calling themselves "Lovers of Zion," they issued a manifesto in which they called for "a home for our country." "It was given to us by the mercy of God; it is ours as registered in the annals of history," they declared. They believed that God had given Palestine to the Jews.

It was at about this same time that modern evangelicals like Darby and Graves began to preach in favor of a restored State of Israel. Following the 1896 publication of a pamphlet entitled "The Jewish State" by Austrian Jew Theodor Herzl, the Lovers of Zion group grew into the Zionist Congress in 1897. But Herzl's pamphlet had certainly not been the first. Jewish longing for a homeland had already reached critical mass earlier in the century. Yehuda Alkalai published "The Third Redemption" as early as 1843. Moses Hess published "Rome and Jerusalem" in 1862, in response to the first successes of modern Italian nationalism. In "Seeking Zion" (1862), Zvi Hirsch Kalischer asked his people to "take to heart the examples of the Italians, the Poles and Hungarians." Another early Zionist leaflet from 1883 demanded, "The slaves of America have been liberated. The Russian serfs have been emancipated. Bulgaria is freed. The time has come to work for the liberation of Israel as well." So, by the time Herzl's publication was circulated, the Jews of Europe had begun to hope that just maybe they, too, might have a chance for a homeland.

If only to keep the number of heartbreaks in the Jewish existence to a manageable level in preceding centuries, the Jews didn't even dare to hope for a homeland. But things began to change. By the time of the First Zionist Congress, the Diaspora Jews were whipped into what, compared to previous centuries, would be a fever pitch. Jews began emigrating to Palestine in record numbers. Some estimates say between 1880 and 1914 over 60,000 Jews arrived in Palestine—mostly from Eastern Europe, where poverty and persecution thrived. The population of Palestine by 1914 is estimated at nearly 100,000 Jews. In 1909, in order to escape the filthy living conditions of Jaffa, an entirely Jewish city—Tel Aviv—was founded on the beach just north of it.

JERUSALEM UNDER THE OTTOMANS

It's important to note just exactly what Jerusalem was prior to the arrival of the Jews to their ancient homeland. Or, for that matter, just what special status the area of Palestine itself occupied in the hearts and minds of its Muslim conquerors during the whole period of rule, from 1517 to 1917. After all, Jerusalem is supposed to be the "third holiest site in Islam." Ted Turner makes that proclamation on an almost weekly basis on CNN while defining the "problem" in the Middle East for millions of mostly uninformed viewers. Under Ottoman rule, the area of Palestine[12]

---

[12] "Palestine" was the Southern Kingdom of Judea until AD 135, when it was renamed by the Romans *Philistina*, or "land of the Philistines," to further aggravate the Jews. The Arabic pronunciation is "Palestine," since they could not pronounce "phi."

was divided into several districts—or sanjaks—such as that of Jerusalem. It was never an important region under the Ottomans, and Jerusalem never occupied the status of even a capital of one of these sanjaks. There was no particular reverence among the Muslim Ottomans for either the Land of Palestine or the City of Jerusalem. To this day a great many Muslims know Jerusalem only by the name *Al Quds*, which means "the farthest Mosque."

The elevation of Jerusalem to "third holiest site" in Islam was largely due to the efforts of the British-appointed Grand Mufti of Jerusalem, Haj Amin al-Husseini, a radical enemy of Jews who exiled himself to Germany to support the Nazis in World War II. Haj Husseini said at a German rally, "Only the Germans know how to deal with the Jews." He was ecstatic about the Nazi death camps. (At the time of this writing, Husseini's grandson is a member of Yasser Arafat's inner Cabinet.)

WORLD WAR I

On November 5, 1914, Britain declared war on Turkey, the home of the Ottoman Empire. The Turks were allies of Germany. Neither the British, nor its allies in France, were in a position to send troops into the Middle East. Britain already had strong interests in the region, controlling Egypt and key points at the southern end of the Arab peninsula, including the Suez Canal. Britain wanted to keep this route open— it was the gateway to Britain's most valued colony, India. This was not an easy job. Much of the Middle

East was in Ottoman hands and had been for centuries. The British realized that if they were to have
any success at all, they needed to cultivate a new
ally—the Arabs. An agreement was drawn up
between the British High Commissioner in Cairo, Sir
Henry McMahon, and Hussein ibn Ali, the Sharif of
Mecca. Ali hoped to be the first leader of an independent Arab state. A letter from McMahon dated
October 24, 1915 started the ball rolling. It was not
clearly written and excluded from any agreement
"portions of Syria lying to the west of Damascus…as
they cannot be said to be purely Arab," but it did
promise the Arabs their own state. "Subject to the
above modifications," the letter stated, "Great Britain
is prepared to recognize and support all regions
within the limits demanded by the Sharif of Mecca."[13]
By this letter, the British promised away Turkish
lands in exchange for Arab aid in defeating Turkey.
Through this and subsequent letters, the areas that
are today Iraq, Saudi Arabia and Egypt were
included in the promise. Not mentioned in any
exchange were the areas of Palestine, which at that
time extended from the Gulf of Aqaba to the southwest across to the Euphrates River in the northwest
corner of what is today Iraq.

THE SYKES—PICOT AGREEMENT

In 1916, Britain and France began negotiating about
what they would do with the Ottoman Empire when

---

[13] Letter dated October 24, 1915, from British High Commissioner
to Cairo.

they won the war. A secret plan, known as the Sykes–Picot Agreement, divided the Ottoman Arab lands into five categories. Some were to be under direct French or British rule, others merely under French or British influence. Finally, a region containing the "holy places"—roughly corresponding to Palestine—was to be under the joint control of both. There was no mention of a separate homeland for the Jews. Neither was there any attempt to honor the understanding given to Hussein. And, a third promise made the following year would complicate the situation even further.

THE BALFOUR DECLARATION

By 1917, things were tough on the British Isles. The war was stalemated in the trenches of France. Battles were being fought with US Civil War vintage weapons—inaccurate and dependent upon gunpowder—which not only often fell short, killing friendly troops, but whose smoke so obscured the battlefield that oftentimes troops would overrun and kill their own positions in the confusion. And, fighting wars is expensive at the best of times. This was not one of those. Money was tight.

At just the right moment in history, a leading Zionist working for the British, Chaim Weitzmann, developed a synthetic substance called acetone and showed how it could be used to create a kind of smokeless gunpowder called "cordite." His invention was received by a "grateful nation." Weitzmann pointed out that grateful as it might be, England was not his nation, but rather, his host nation. He asked the Crown for a nation for his own people. The problem was turned over to Lord Arthur Balfour. Balfour saw several advantages for Britain in acceding to Weitzmann's request. First, he needed the support of the wealthy Jews inside Britain, especially Lord Lionel Rothschild, a wealthy Jew and prominent banker. Secondly, it would be in Britain's interests to have a state friendly to Britain in the eastern Mediterranean region. Thirdly, largely as a result of the growing sympathy for a Jewish state brought on thanks to Darby and the rising tide of evangelical Christianity, there was public support for the concept in Parliament. Lord Balfour then sent his famous letter, known to history as "The Balfour Declaration," that promised a Jewish homeland in Palestine.

CONTRADICTORY MANDATES

By the end of the Great War, Britain found itself in the position of having promised all things to all people, and now it was time to deliver. The McMahon–Hussein Agreement gave the land east of Damascus to Hussein of Mecca. The Sikes–Picot Agreement divided it up between Britain and France. And, the Balfour Declaration gave Palestine to the Jews.

The French and British solved their differences by the simple expedient of dividing up the territory by drawing borders, freehand, over the map of the Middle East. The French created Syria and Lebanon.

The British carved Iraq and Transjordan out of what had been Mesopotamia. But when it came to Palestine, the Arabs dug in their heels and demanded that as well. Arab hopes had been raised by McMahon's declaration of support for Arab independence, which the Arabs now claimed encompassed the whole Middle East.

The lack of historical understanding on the part of the British and French diplomats involved is staggering. They drew boundary lines that artificially divided ancient tribal lands and divided tribes into nation–states. The legacy of these "diplomats" to future generations was a Middle East in a perpetual state of war. Now, *that's* diplomacy!

THE GREAT BRITISH ADVANCE BACKWARD

The Balfour Declaration and the support it received in the British government greatly annoyed the Arabs. Even Winston Churchill had spoken eloquently in favor of keeping Lord Balfour's commitment: "It is manifestly right that the Jews, who are scattered all over the world, should have a national home where some of them might be reunited. Where else could this be but in this land of Palestine, with which for more than 3,000 years they have been intimately and profoundly associated? We think it will be good for the world, good for the Jews, and good for Britain."

But it was not good for the Arabs. And they, as it so happens, have most of the proven oil reserves. In

1921, at the San Remo conference, *the British said they had misspoken, and did not intend for the WHOLE of Palestine to become a Jewish State.* They proposed instead to divide Palestine into two states, one Arab, and one Jewish. This was an outright lie and marked the beginning of constant concessions to the Arabs' increasing demands.

THE PARTITION PLANS

The British proposal to divide the area into two states was well received by the Jews. Chaim Weitzmann—who went on to be Israel's first president—enthusiastically discussed the plan with King Faisal Hussein of Iraq, who initially gave his blessing, then withdrew his support in 1929. But if the Arabs had accepted the 1919 plan, the Jewish minority may well have been absorbed into an Arab Palestinian State. And that was not God's plan for His people.

The Peel Commission in 1937 offered a similar "two nations–one state" proposal. Again, it was accepted by the Jews and rejected by the Arabs. Again, the irony is, had the Arabs accepted it, they would have won the battle for land over which they are currently fighting. And, they would have won without firing a shot and with the enthusiastic support of the Jews.

The Woodhead Report of 1938 proposed an even smaller region of Jewish autonomy. Again, the Arabs rejected it; the Jews supported it, although somewhat more reluctantly.

The White Paper of 1939, offered by the British, was much more pro Arab than any previous offer. At the time, the British were trying to win Arab sympathies away from the German Nazi Party. The White Paper curtailed Jewish immigration, cut back Jewish settlements—in fact, it was little more than a tacit recognition that Jews actually physically existed on the land. Amazingly, the Arabs rejected even this plan, which gives insight into what they really want. And what they really want is the total obliteration of any Jewish presence in what they continue to call Palestine.

The UN Partition Plan of 1947 offered by the UN gave a tiny portion of the land to Israel, the remainder to the Arabs, and declared Jerusalem an open city. This, too, was rejected by the Arabs.

The first time any partition plan ever offered by anyone was even looked at seriously by the Arab side was in 1968. That was after they had lost the West Bank and city of Jerusalem to Israel following their most recent attempt to wipe the Jewish State off the face of the earth. Then they wanted to reconsider the White Paper of 1939, or the UN Partition Plan, or whatever. But this mellow mood did not appear until they knew they'd never get it any other way.

This is not rational conduct, folks. These people are doing just what God said they would do exactly when He said they would do it. This is Bible prophecy coming alive and functioning before us, with the whole world as witnesses.

A terrible catastrophe is about to fall on all the Muslim nations that have attacked Israel. The warning is clearly predicted in Ezekiel 36:1–10, but none of these people are listening. What a tragedy!

CHAPTER 3

TERRIBLE TRAGEDY AND RAY OF HOPE

For 2,000 years, the Jews lived in host countries during the Diaspora. They were used to being scapegoats for whatever ills befell their host nations. They were a kind of national "Cinderella" who, unlike the fairy tale, never got to go to the ball. They were blamed for famines, plagues, crop failures, bad weather and economic downturns. They were systematically expelled—as in Spain in 1492— where they were forced to leave behind their accumulated possessions and wealth that had been built up for generations. For over 18 centuries they were mercilessly pursued by Christians and Muslims alike, fulfilling the words of Moses previously quoted.

NO NATION HAS EVER BEEN SO CLEARLY FOREWARNED

But Moses predicted an end to the Jewish unbelief and foretold their regathering. Ezekiel predicted their initial partial gathering in unbelief before the Tribulation. But here, Moses predicts their total regathering after GOD pours out the Spirit of grace and supplication upon the remnant in the Tribulation:

> "So it shall be when all of these things have come upon you, the blessing and the curse which I have set before you, and you call them to mind in all nations where the LORD you God has banished you, and you return to the LORD your God and obey Him with all your heart and soul according to all that I command you today, you and your sons, then the LORD your God will restore you from captivity, and have compassion on you, and will gather you again from all the peoples where the LORD your God has scattered you. If your outcasts are at the ends of the earth, from there the LORD your God will gather you, and from there He will bring you back."[14]

The purpose, of course, was so that the heathen nations would recognize that the blessings of Israel were God–given, and thereby God would be revealed to the nations through Israel. But the promise was a two–edged sword. If the seed of Abraham did not

---

[14] Deuteronomy 30:1–4 NASB.

remain faithful to God, then Israel would be cursed above all nations—which also reveals the arm of God to the heathen nations of the world. In either case, God would be revealed through the seed of Abraham. That was God's plan.

> "Thus says the LORD, 'Behold, I am sending upon them the sword, famine, and pestilence, and I will make them like split–open figs that cannot be eaten due to rottenness. And I will pursue them with the sword, with famine and with pestilence; and I will make them a terror to all the kingdoms of the earth, to be a curse, and a horror, and a hissing, and a reproach among all the nations where I have driven them, because they have not listened to My words,' declares the LORD, 'which I sent to them again and again by My servants the prophets; but you did not listen,' declares the LORD."[15]

If ever in history there was a nation that could be characterized as a reproach, or a curse or a horror, or a "hissing," it would be the nation of Israel. The very word "Jew" is a slang term for a miser, so indelible is the identification that another way of describing a negotiation for a lower price in a sale is often called "trying to jew him down."

PROMISES OF HOPE

No nation in history was ever so thoroughly "scattered" among the nations of the world than was the

---

[15] Jeremiah 29:17–19 NASB.

seed of Abraham. Yet, always, a tiny remnant remained in the Land of Promise, exactly as God promised.

> "However, I shall leave a remnant, for you will have those who escaped the sword among the nations when you are scattered among the countries. Then those of you who escape will remember Me among the nations to which they will be carried captive, how I have been hurt by their adulterous hearts which turned away from Me, and by their eyes, which played the harlot after their idols; and they will loathe themselves in their own sight for the evils which they have committed, for all their abominations. Then they will know that I am the Lord; I have not said in vain that I would inflict this disaster on them."[16]

The Jews were indeed scattered, starting with the Babylonian destruction. The remnant that later returned remained in the land under occupation. After the Babylonians, the Media–Persians came. Then came Alexander and the Greeks, followed later by the Romans. After the majority of Israel rejected their Messiah, they were utterly scattered into what is known as the Diaspora. Those in exile never forgot the promise of God that they would one–day return to their ancient home. S. Y. Agnon, in a Nobel Prize acceptance speech in 1966, expressed that hope eloquently: "Through a historical catastrophe—the destruction of Jerusalem by the Emperor of Rome, I

---

[16] Ezekiel 6:8–10 NASB.

was born in one of the cities of the Diaspora. But I always deemed myself as one who was really born in Jerusalem."

But, nothing in their long history prepared the Jews of the Diaspora for the Holocaust.

THE NAZI MADNESS

Even the long–unbroken history of the Jewish people as the eternal scapegoat failed to prepare them for what the Nazis had in store for them, beginning with Hitler's rise to power in 1933. It began slowly, at first. Jews were segregated even further than what they were used to. Laws were passed making it a crime for a Jewish doctor to treat an Aryan, or a Jewish lawyer to practice law in an Aryan court or defend an Aryan defendant. Special taxes were imposed on Jews. Certain areas were forbidden to Jews. Jews were expelled from universities and schools.

By the time of the infamous Kristalnacht—or "Night of the Broken Glass"—some Jews began to recognize their danger, and quietly abandoned all they owned and fled the country. But many remained, still unconvinced of the mortal danger that awaited them. To them, this was just another passing anti–Semitic phase. Many held this view almost up to the very moment that they were herded naked into the "showers" at Auschwitz, Buchenwald, Bergen–Belsen and Treblinka, *etc*. Millions died in this manner, millions—but not all.

MIDWIFE TO THE BIRTH OF A NATION

Those who survived were a very different brand of Jews than the world had seen in two millennia. They were tough, they were determined, and they would not be dissuaded from their goal by the threat of a mere 650 million Muslims in the neighborhood. As terrible as it was, in a very real way, the Holocaust was the catalyst for the rebirth of the State of Israel. Like all Satan's previous attempts to thwart the will of God, his effort to use Adolf Hitler and his henchmen to eradicate God's Chosen People merely revealed the awesome power "to work all things together for good." The Jews of the Holocaust cried, "Never again!" and the promise God recorded in Chapter 37 of Ezekiel became a reality. It is the ultimate irony of history that the Nazi madness served as the midwife to the birth of modern Israel.

THE WORLD'S MOMENTARY TWINGE OF GUILT

In order for the infant nation to have even a ghost of a chance, it needed strong support from the great nations of the world. History shows that support would never have existed without the Holocaust. There were many places in the world in the first half of the 20th century where Jews were relatively well treated—the United States, Britain, France (to some degree) and most of Western Europe.

We Americans like to think we have always been a haven for Jews like we have been for Poles, Frenchmen, Italians, *etc.* Jews in America have excelled in the entertainment industry, banking, the law, politics or any other vocation they chose—but not because America gave them a free ride.

Groucho Marx was one of the most famous and beloved comedians of this century—an icon in American culture. Yet when he attempted to join a country club near his home, his application was rejected because he was a Jew. His reaction was typical. He quipped, "I wouldn't join any club that would have me as a member." Prior to the Holocaust, there is very little reason to think that even the United States would have supported a Jewish state.

History reveals that the Western world stood idly by—even though they had some knowledge of what was happening in the Nazi camps. Not a single extermination camp was ever touched by Allied bombs!

THE USA'S MOST SHAMEFUL DECISION

The saddest example of Allied apathy to the plight of European Jewry is found in the story of the St. Louis. On May 13, 1939, that ship, carrying 930 Jewish refugees—men, women and children—set sail for America. Most had documents that entitled them to land in the USA. All had documents that would have allowed them to land in Cuba. Cuba allowed 22 refugees to disembark on their soil. The USA refused to accept a single one.

The St. Louis languished off the coast of Florida before finally having to return Jewish passengers to Europe and the waiting arms of their Nazi exterminators. Some of the Nazi leaders pleaded this incident as justification for their participation in the

Holocaust at their trials for war crimes at Nuremberg. They reasoned that, after all, we didn't want the Jews either.

Some of Britain's wartime activities where Jews and the camps were concerned bordered on outright collaboration. Other Allies, like France, actively participated in the rounding up of innocent French citizens (who happened to be Jews) and shipped them to the camps in the rest of Europe, fully aware of their ultimate fate. They didn't know it at the time, but by their activities they were writing a check that in 1948 Israel presented for payment. Faced by the representative of their shame, unwilling to admit any guilt, they had no choice but to heed the Jewish call of "never again" and grant them membership in the assembly of nations.

CHAPTER 4

PROVIDENCE IN STRANGE PLACES

THE YALTA CONFERENCE

In February 1945, the leaders of the soon–to–be

victorious Allied powers met in Yalta, on the Crimean

Peninsula in the Ukraine. Their purpose, according

to a joint communiqué issued by the Allies, was

"to destroy German militarism and Nazism so as to

ensure that Germany will never again be able to

disturb the peace of the world"; to "bring all war

criminals to just and swift punishment"; and to

"exact reparation in kind for the destruction

wrought by the Germans."

What it really did was divide the world in two. On one side was the Communist East. On the other side was the capitalist West. The Allied leaders who re–drew the map of Europe were Franklin D. Roosevelt, Winston Churchill and Josef Stalin. Ostensibly, the plan was to create three zones of influence, an American zone, a British zone, and a Russian zone.

At the conference, it was decided to extend the occupation zones to include France. France had been conquered in 1940, and as such wasn't really "victorious," but rather, it was liberated, but the Western powers had already begun to distrust Stalin. The invitation extended to France was a concession made to Churchill, who wanted to limit Soviet expansion. It didn't work.

It was at Yalta that the United Nations was actually born. The Allied leaders recognized that World War II had ushered in a genuine New World Order. The unanswered question was, who would run it? Stalin's world didn't appeal to the Western leaders, especially Churchill. Rather than taking a chance on losing all of it, the Western leaders signed away half of Europe.

US President Franklin Delano Roosevelt, as we now know, was seriously ill during this conference and seemed to capitulate to almost all of Joseph Stalin's demands. Churchill apparently saved the Western nations from signing even more away to the Soviet Union.

TECHNOLOGY AND THE WAR

World War II forced a rapid technological revolution. On August 6, 1945, in the closing days of World War

Two, a lone American B–29 bomber appeared in the skies over Japan.

It was only three years before, on April 18, 1942, that Col. Jimmy Doolittle had led the first bombing raid against Japan. The Doolittle raid was the first carrier–based launch of heavy bombers in history. The target—Tokyo—suffered little real damage. It was much more significant as a propaganda victory, showing the folks back home that Japan was not invulnerable to attack. Still, the weapons were relatively primitive, and only a handful of men survived the raid.

The August 6, 1945, raid was different. In just over three years, technological advances made necessary by the war moved the world into a new fearful era. The B–29 (named Enola Gay after pilot Paul Tibbets' mother) bore as little resemblance to the eight–year–older B–17 bomber as a Model–A Ford bears to a new Ford Taurus. And the Enola Gay carried a new and devastating payload equal to thousands of times the combined payload of the Doolittle raid.

This time, the target was Hiroshima, and the payload was the atom bomb. The destruction it caused was utterly shocking. Within only days of the attack, the Japanese government surrendered unconditionally. There were solid reasons for using the Bomb. The decision spared the US the risk of an invasion that would have cost millions of American lives and possibly 50% of the population. And, in so doing, brought the world into the Atomic Age.

THE BERLIN BLOCKADE AND THE COLD WAR

The atom bomb opened a new era in diplomacy. The United States catapulted overnight into its role of first among nations. As long as the US possessed the only working nuclear weapons, war with the Americans was unthinkable! For too many nations, especially the Stalinist Soviet Union, that was a temporary situation. The Soviets, British and French all embarked on separate programs to develop their own nuclear weapons. Soon, the nuclear club had four members. Red China would eventually be the fifth.

NUCLEAR MUSCLE BEACH

The era of atomic muscle flexing officially kicked off as a result of the breakdown of the Western–Soviet coalition against Hitler's Germany and its allies during World War II. Both design and misunderstanding played vital roles in the origin and development of the conflict.

Initially, the central issue was the extent and form of Soviet control over Eastern Europe, which Joseph Stalin deemed indispensable for Soviet security. His failure to define the limits of Soviet security needs, compounded by Western failure to make clear the limits of Western interest in the area, eventually led to a mutual effort to expand the respective spheres of influence as far as possible.

In contravention to World War II agreements calling for political self–determination, the Soviet Union proceeded to impose Communist regimes on all the nations of Eastern Europe. When the Communists seemed to be winning the civil war in Greece, the Soviet Union simultaneously applied pressure on Turkey. In 1947, the US adopted a policy of containment. Enunciated in the Truman Doctrine, the policy affirmed American intent to oppose communism, if necessary by force, wherever it might attempt to expand.

THE MARSHALL PLAN

The Marshall Plan focused on internal recovery of Western Europe as the main protection against such expansion. The Soviet Union responded to the Truman Doctrine and the Marshall Plan with the formation of a new Communist International Union (the Cominform) and a tightening of its control of Eastern Europe. The United States then resolved to strengthen West Germany against communism.

THE BIRTH OF THE EU

In February 1948, a plan for the economic merger of the British and US occupation zones went into effect following its acceptance by the Germans in those zones. A conference, attended by representatives of the United States, Belgium, the Netherlands, Luxembourg, France, and Great Britain, was held in London to discuss the eventual political and economic merger of the French, British, and US occupation zones. In reaction to this violation of the Yalta and Potsdam agreements, the Soviet delegation withdrew from the Four–Power Allied Control Council and took steps to establish a Soviet–dominated East

German state.

On June 24, 1948, an agreement by those nations of the London Conference resulted in the creation of a West German state and the establishment of a West German currency by the Western occupying powers.

In response, the Soviets banned all rail traffic between Berlin and West Germany. Because water and roadway transportation into the city had been suspended by an earlier Soviet action, the British and US occupation authorities organized a system of air transport, known as the Berlin airlift, to supply the Western– occupied sectors of the city.

AND THUS, THE BERLIN CRISIS

"In 1948, under savage and provocative Russian pressure in Berlin, the US refused to abandon Europe's helpless peoples. With that decision, the US accepted the risk of war. Major General William H. Tunner's airlift blazed a roaring, dramatic demonstration of US determination across Europe's troubled skies. Not only to Berliners but also to the world, the Berlin Airlift was the symbol of the year: the US meant business. (Last week, completing six months of operation, US and British planes had carried a total of 700,172 tons in 96,640 flights.)" [17]

BASIC EFFECTS OF THE COLD WAR

The Berlin Airlift, that started the Cold War, occurred at a most strategic point in history, as far as God's

---

[17] *TIME*, January 3, 1949.

plan for the last generation is concerned. At roughly the same point in history in which the West recognized the danger presented by Stalin and his hordes, a new democracy in the Middle East was struggling for recognition. Each side wanted control of the oil rich region, and many of the Zionists who founded Israel were historically Russian Jews sympathetic to both Marxist and Communist ideology. On the other hand, the United States had always been the most hospitable of the Diaspora countries. Although the Russian Jews were somewhat utopian politically, they remembered how cruelly they had been treated in Russia.

Against this political backdrop, David Ben Gurion asked the UN to recognize the new State of Israel. Either the United States or Russia could have aborted the infant nation by use of its veto power in the UN Security Council. But both immediately recognized the new state. Russia hoped Israel would become a new client state in the Middle East. The United States intended to prevent that from happening.

In a very real sense, the Cold War was as essential an element in the realization of Ezekiel's vision of the dry bones as was the Holocaust. No matter how hard Satan tried to extinguish the Jews, his every effort worked against him. The GOD of the impossible indeed "causes all things to work together for good, for those who are called according to His purpose."

The Cold War also enabled the USSR to build the most formidable arsenal of weapons of mass destruction in history. That arsenal is now equipping the

Muslim confederacy for their predicted war with Israel, just as Ezekiel predicted the Russian sons of Magog would do.

It was this same arsenal that forced Europe to do by peaceful means what it had not been able to do since the disintegration of the Roman Empire, Phase One. In response to the threat of Soviet expansionism, the Europeans began formulating agreements like the Treaty of Rome, the Benelux Treaty, the Coal and Steel Pact, *etc.* Those treaties were the foundation of the modern European superstate—which I believe is the precursor of the predicted Revived Roman Empire, Phase 2. It was elaborately predicted—and it is happening now!

CHAPTER 5

WHAT SHALL BE THE SIGN OF YOUR COMING?

SOME REMINISCENCES OF A REMARKABLE MAN

The old man gazed down at the document before him. He wasn't that old at 62—not really, but years of deprivation and hardship had added 20 years to his appearance.

His shock of white hair, balding in front, stuck out on the sides, made him look for all the world like a mad scientist. *Twelve more hours,* he thought. He wondered how many other men saw as clearly—in advance—the historical connotations of the events they would soon participate in. And in his case, the event was 2,500 years in the making, but he was the man who would take the blame—or the credit—for what would certainly change the face of the world forever. *Ahh,* he thought, *there will only be blame. That's how it's always been.* In the outer room, he could hear the arguments that had been going on all night. He retired to his room, only partly to review the foundational document before him. His real reason was to get away from the cacophony of voices all struggling to be heard amid the nervous clamor. It was a ridiculous argument anyway, but it kept everybody busy and gave everyone an equal sense of participation in the birth of a nation. He could hear them through the walls tossing around possible names for the new State: "Zion!" "Greater Zion!" "Judah!" "Judea!"

Ahh, he sighed, *whenever you have three Jews in a room, you have five opinions.* He thought briefly about a conversation he had in April 1936, with George Antonius, the historian, and a leading Arab theoretician of his day. Antonius was in favor of—perhaps it would be more accurate to say he was not totally against—the establishment of a tiny Jewish enclave along the coast. But he insisted there must be a limit to Jewish immigration. David Ben–Gurion told him then: "It was not by caprice that we return to this country. For us it is a question of survival, of life and death. We have come here to stay whether there will or will not be Arab–Jewish understanding. Riots will not stop us. If we have the choice between riots in Germany, Poland or in any other country, and riots in Palestine, then we prefer riots in Palestine. Still, I ask, what is better for both our sides—to fight, or to help one another?"

As he thought about the battle before him, he remembered the look on the faces of those Arabs present during his conversation with Antonius. He knew the Arab would have but one answer—Jihad, a holy war.

Ben–Gurion returned to the document before him. It was his country's declaration of independence. He shuddered with pride at the words "his country" and "independence."

A BRIEF HISTORY OF "THE SON OF A LION"

Born David Grein in 1886 in Czarist Poland, he was transfixed at a very early age with the dream of a homeland for the Jews. In 1906, as word came of the latest czarist pogrom against his people, he was seized with an irresistible urge. Carrying only a small knapsack, he traveled by fourth–class train to Odessa, continued in steerage across the Black Sea and down the eastern shore of the Mediterranean.

Three weeks after he left Plonsk, he was finally rowed ashore onto the rocky port of Jaffa. He didn't like Jaffa—it was dirty and depressing. He continued on foot—not even stopping overnight—to the nearby colony of Petach Tikva. It was, at that time, a small village of a few hundred souls. A muddy path led through its single street. Ben–Gurion spent his first night in a Spartan workers' hostel, a wooden shack with straw mats. He remembered his thoughts that day. My heart overflowed with happiness that day as if I had entered the realm of joy. A dream was celebrating its victory. *I am in Eretz Israel, in a Hebrew village in Eretz Israel, in a Hebrew village called Petach Tikva, "Gate of Hope."*

It was during those days that he did what most immigrants did; he gave himself a new Hebrew name. He chose *Ben–Gurion,* which means "son of a lion." The name came to fit his courageous spirit.

It had been an arduous journey, but nothing compared to the hardships suffered by many others on their way to my country, he thought.

Then he smiled as his thoughts returned to the momentous event about to happen. "My country," he muttered. Then he unknowingly fulfilled many ancient prophecies by writing in the name "Israel" at the top of the document.

WHEN JEWS BECAME ISRAELIS

He thought again about the certainty of war this proclamation was about to bring. *But,* he thought, *what else can we do? It's better for us to die fighting for a country than to die as victims because we have no country.* This kind of thinking formed the indomitable spirit that produced the kind of warriors in Israel not seen since the days of King David. David Ben–Gurion infected others with his do–or–die courage.

Ben–Gurion's thoughts once again returned to the document before him. He choked with emotion at the words "his country" and "independence." Indeed, he was about to make the country happen.

THE REBIRTH OF ISRAEL

On May 14, 1948—2,500 years after Babylon captured Jerusalem and destroyed the First Temple, 1,878 years after the Romans destroyed Jerusalem and the Second Temple and scattered the Jews into the four corners of the earth—David Ben–Gurion declared the new state. The Americans immediately recognized the State of Israel. The Russians also recognized the new state, not wanting to risk losing a possible client state in the region. Reluctantly, the United Nations accepted Israel's declaration of Independence in accordance with the 1947 UN Partition plan. That plan gave a tiny sliver of land along to the coast to Israel, the Gaza Strip and the West Bank to the Arabs, and declared Jerusalem an open city under international control.

THE WAR OF ANNIHILATION

The very next day, on May 15, 1948, five well–equipped Muslim armies attacked the tiny new State of Israel from all sides.

The British–trained and equipped Arab Legion of Jordan attacked and captured the power station at Naharayim. An Iraqi expeditionary force tried to ford the Jordan River in the area of Gesher. They were held back for a full week by the poorly armed settlers of Gesher. The Iraqis finally withdrew, choosing to cross the river at a ford held by the Jordanians.

The Syrians actually began their attack on the night of May 14. They unleashed a devastating barrage of heavy artillery against the poorly armed settlements south of the Sea of Galilee.

PREMATURE RADIO ANNOUNCEMENTS

Arab radios announced with euphoric glee that the "War of Annihilation" had begun! The Arab Legions numbered more than 650,000 men. British mercenary officers of great renown led some of the Arab armies. All Arab armies were armed with the most modern of weapons and air power of the time.

The Jews, on the other hand, had only 45,000 "troops," most of whom were guerrilla fighters from the Haganah, Palmach, or members of the Irgun and Stern groups. Under the British Mandate, it was a crime punishable by death for a Jew to carry a firearm—although Arabs carried weapons openly. As a result, the new Jewish army had very little with which to defend itself. Chaim Herzog, the Jewish historian, estimates the total armament at the Haganah's disposal was 10,500 rifles, 3,500 light submachine guns, 775 light machine guns, 34 three-inch mortars, and 670 two-inch mortars. And, worst of all, they only had sufficient ammunition for three days' fighting.

The Palmach—the "Israeli Army," for want of a more descriptive term—was able to arm only two out of three of its fighters. Against the Arab Legion's modern jet air force, Israel had 20 unarmed Piper Cubs. The Arabs also controlled the only landing strips in Palestine.

WHO REALLY CAUSED THE PALESTINIAN REFUGEES?

Weeks before the war, Arab families were encouraged to abandon their homes and flee to the Arab countries. They were assured that within a matter of weeks, they would be allowed to return and reclaim their homes—and also the homes of the massacred Jews. Although the new Israeli government pleaded with them to stay and fight together for a common homeland, all but a handful crossed over into Jordan to wait for total victory against the Jews. They expected to return home as soon as the hated Jew was slaughtered. Instead, after the war was lost, their "brother" hosts kept them in miserable refugee camps and did nothing to help them.

THE WAR OF INDEPENDENCE

The Arabs fought a very different Jew than those who went meekly into Hitler's death camps, or lined up naked in front of ditches to be machine-gunned by members of the SS Einsatzgruppen.

Outnumbered by more than 100 to one, and hopelessly outgunned, these survivors of the death camps, of countless persecutions in the Muslim countries, and of the hardships that life in Palestine had to offer shocked not just the Arab armies, but the entire world.

Many Israelis charged into battle without a weapon to take one from the dead body of a fallen enemy. A few Jews from outside the country flew in on a wing and a prayer with obsolete German Messerschmit fighters purchased from Czechoslovakia. With these planes and some cavalier volunteer pilots, they cleared the skies of enemy planes and turned back an Egyptian armored corps in the Southern Gaza Strip.

With a determination rarely seen in any war before or since, the Jews met every onslaught. It cost them dearly—10% of the total population of the new Israeli State fell in battle. But when the dust cleared, the Israelis controlled all the land set aside for them by the original Mandate plus half the city of Jerusalem. On June 11, 1949, the Arabs withdrew, and the Israeli State became a fact.

At the beginning, it looked hopeless for the outnumbered and outgunned Jews. The Arabs were justified in their conviction of an easy victory. But some of the rabbis proclaimed God's promises from the Torah to the beleaguered men, **"Five of you will chase a hundred, and a hundred of you will chase ten thousand, and your enemies will fall before you by the sword"** (Leviticus 26:8).

IF THIS WASN'T A MIRACLE, WHAT IS?

The land of Israel became the land of the Jews, by miracle, if you please. Their victory is inexplicable apart from the unseen intervention of the Hand of God. God has a Plan for the last days. A restored land of Israel, homeland to the Jewish people, is the key element in His plan, and the very existence of Israel bears testimony to it. The old rabbis remembered, and even the atheist immigrants from Russia took heed to the words of the prophet Isaiah: **"Remember the former things long past, for I am God, and there is no other; I am God, and there is no one like Me, declaring the end from the beginning and from ancient times things which have not been done, saying, My purpose will be established, and I will accomplish all My good pleasure..."** (Isaiah 46:8–10).

The miraculous birth of Israel was just the beginning. So much so, in fact, that most rabbis proclaim this time as the beginning of the Messianic era.

God wants the world to know that His promises concerning His chosen people are His promises, not merely legends in an old Book. By their very survival, the Jews prove God is exactly who He says He is, and, His counsel shall indeed stand, and He will do all His pleasure. The birth of Israel sets a pattern that is drawing us inexorably toward the end of days and the Day of the Lord. Israel fought five wars in its short 50 years: The War of Independence, the Sinai Wars, the 1956 Suez Crisis, the Six–Day War and the Yom Kippur War. In each war, Israel ended up with just a little bit more of the territory God promised to "Abraham's seed forever."

To date, every Muslim effort to cast the Israelis out of their Promised Land has resulted in Israel gaining more of that very land.

THE SIX–DAY MIRACLE WAR

At 11:00 AM on June 5, 1967, the Jordanian army launched a barrage of artillery and small arms fire from positions along the winding armistice line against targets inside Israel. The principal targets of the Jordanian gunners were the cities of Tel Aviv and West Jerusalem. During the 1948 War of Independence, Israel captured the western side of the city, but East Jerusalem remained in Jordanian hands. The assault was intended to recapture the entire city, and hopefully (from the Arab perspective), ultimately drive the Jews into the sea. At the very least, it was intended to force Israel back to the original borders of the UN Partition Plan, while leaving the Arabs in control of all of Jerusalem.

The Israeli Defense Forces were able to repulse the invaders and eventually captured East Jerusalem, the entire West Bank area of the Jordan River, the Golan Heights, the Gaza Strip and all of the Sinai. These territories gave Israel a "buffer zone" that was desperately needed. For the first time, Israel had truly defensible borders. These are still the most strategic territories in the entire country. Without them, Israel would be, at its narrowest, about 11 miles wide. But more importantly, from a prophetic perspective, Israel once again sovereignly controlled the entire city of Jerusalem for the first time in 2500 years. Jesus predicted about this: **"They will fall by the edge of the sword, and will be led captive into all the nations; and Jerusalem will be trampled under foot by the Gentiles UNTIL the times of the Gentiles be fulfilled"** (Luke 21:24). This event should have warned us Gentiles that our time is getting very short.

JERUSALEM—ISRAEL'S CHIEF JOY

Despite Arab claims to the contrary, Jerusalem is the city of David, and it is, without question, historically a Jewish city. The Palestinian Authority has done all it can to cast doubt on Israel's claim. One PA propagandist even published a paper saying that all the archeological finds that support the Jewish claim to the city are forgeries. But he failed to come up with a good propaganda story that would explain away a 2,500–year–old lament that proves beyond doubt the historicity of Israel's claim to the ancient City of God.

The Psalmist wrote: **"If I forget you, O Jerusalem, may my right hand forget her skill. May my tongue cleave to the roof of my mouth, if I do not remember you, if I do not exalt Jerusalem above my chief joy."**[18] Indeed, the name Jerusalem is woven throughout the Old and New Testaments. It is presented as the center of all acceptable worship of God. It alone is called by God "His city."

Although the Arabs say that Jerusalem is the third holiest site in Islam, as we saw in Chapter Two, that just isn't supported by the historical record. Jerusalem may be important to the Arab cause politically; its ranking in religious importance is somewhat murkier. The Muslim claim to the city is based on the fact that Muhammad rode to heaven aboard a winged steed from the area now occupied by the Dome of the Rock. *The Koran doesn't actually say the trip originated at Temple Mount.* The Koran doesn't even mention Jerusalem—not even once!

---

[18] Psalm 137:5, 6 NASB.

JERUSALEM—THE ONLY CITY GOD CLAIMS IS HIS

Israel's claim to the city is supported by the Old Testament, but it is given even greater authenticity by Jesus Christ Himself. The mere possession of the city by the Israelis is an indicator of the times in which we live. In describing the signs that would precede His return, Jesus gave the long-term prospects for the city, from its destruction by Titus and the Roman legions in AD 70 to the last generation in history: **"They will fall by the edge of the sword, and will be led captive into all the nations; and Jerusalem will be trampled under foot by the Gentiles until the times of the Gentiles be fulfilled."**[19]

The **"times of the Gentiles"**—of which the Church Age is a part—is fulfilled with the Rapture of the Church, and sets the stage for the 70th Week of Daniel, or the Tribulation Period. In other words, the Jews must be in possession of the entire city of Jerusalem before that event could occur. That isn't to say that the Tribulation Period begins with the possession of the city. But, it does mean that the prophetic time-clock stalled in 1948, and did not resume again until the pivotal event on June 6, 1967, when for the first time in 2500 years, Jews once again had sovereign control of Jerusalem and have maintained it.

---

[19] Luke 21:24 NASB.

ISRAEL—THE PIVOTAL POINT OF BIBLE PROPHECY

To this point, most of our focus has remained on Israel. Israel remains the linchpin—that pivotal event upon which all the other prophecies for the last days are dependent. The three remaining elements of end-time prophecy are the global economy, the global religion and the global government. Israel plays a key role in the development of all three. All three have a role to play in the last days—a role that they could not begin until Israel was once again a nation of Jews in their own land. Now that the nation of Israel has regained her land as God promised, a bigger picture begins to emerge.

THE 70 WEEKS OF DANIEL

Among the Hebrews taken captive by King Nebuchadnezzar of Babylon in 586 BC was a young, devout Jew named Daniel. There are many books detailing the life and times of Daniel the Prophet, so we won't attempt to chronicle in a few paragraphs events that deserve their own volume. Instead, we'll deal with Daniel's vision of the 70 weeks. Daniel was given a vision by an angel sent from God, detailing future geopolitical history in advance. The angel spoke of two distinct futures—one detailing the future of Israel, the other dealing with the gentile world. The Jewish future laid out a specific time line:

> "Seventy weeks have been decreed for your peo-
> ple and your holy city, to finish the transgression,
> to make an end of sin, to make atonement for

iniquity, to bring in everlasting righteousness, to seal up vision and prophecy, and to anoint the most holy place."[20]

In this one verse is a synopsis of Jewish history, from Daniel's day to the Return of Jesus Christ. **"Seventy weeks have been decreed for your people and your holy city,"** Daniel was told. The Jews measured time in units, as did the Greeks. In the West, we still use the Greek designation "decade" to denote a period of ten years. The Hebrews measured by sevens, rather than tens like the Greeks. So the Hebrew equivalent to a decade of ten years was the Hebrew *shabua*, or "*week*," a period of seven years. In addition, they also were commanded to keep a sabbath year as well as a sabbath day. It was the failure to keep seventy sabbath years that brought God's judgment upon them.

Seventy of these "weeks" indicates a period of 490 years. Note that the 70 weeks were determined upon Daniel's people, the Jews and the Holy City, Jerusalem.

The purpose of this allotment of time is to finish the transgression, and to make an end of sins.[21] Israel's national reconciliation with God will take place when the people of Israel **"shall look upon Me whom they have pierced; and they will mourn for Him, as one mourns for an only son...."** This occurs just before Jesus returns visibly at the Battle of Armageddon.

---

[20] Daniel 9:24 NASB.

[21] Daniel 9:24—Literally, "490 years are allotted..."

HOW ACCURATE IS DANIEL?

The accuracy of Daniel's prophecies is one of the reasons that so many skeptics advance the theory that the Book of Daniel was written around 162 BC by a Hellenist Jew named Judas Maccabaeus. The skeptic cannot reconcile Daniel's precision in any other way—short of the obvious acceptance of God's inspiration, an apparently unacceptable choice. But the following aspect of the prophecy cannot be explained away by late dating.

THE FIRST 69 WEEKS

Daniel's vision, in particular that part dealing with the first 69 weeks, intrigued Sir Robert Anderson, a retired Scotland Yard Inspector of the late 19th century. Daniel 9:25 predicts: **"Know and discern that from the issuing of a decree to restore and build Jerusalem until Messiah the Prince there will be seven weeks and sixty-two weeks...."**

In other words, using the issuance of the only decree that authorized the rebuilding of both the city of Jerusalem and the Temple as a starting point (given by Artaxerxes Longimanus of Persia), 483 years later should bring us to the time of Jesus.

Sir Robert calculated these seven weeks, plus 62 weeks or 483 years (69 x 7 = 483). Virtually every fair authority to examine them since has confirmed his calculations. Others, like Hoehner's *Chronological Aspects of the Life of Christ,* have carried Anderson's calculations even farther.

HOW ACCURATE IS PROPHECY?

Most agree that the only decree that fits the prophecy was the decree issued by King Artaxerxes to Nehemiah. The Bible records the date as "the month Nisan, in the twentieth year of King Artaxerxes" (Nehemiah 2:1) or, the 20th year of his reign on the first day of the month of Nisan. The Greenwich Observatory confirmed the date as March 5, 444 BC. Anderson's calculations were among the first to recognize the Hebrew lunar calendar; it has a 360–day year, 12 months of 30 days each.

Anderson used a simple conversion process. The length of a year varied by calendar, but a day was still a day. By dividing 483 years by 360 days we find the 69 weeks equal exactly 173,880 days. From 444 BC to AD 33 is 477 years (according to our calendar), but AD 1 and 1 BC were the same year, so the actual length of time was 476 years. Multiplying 476 years by 365.24219879 (allowing for leap years, *etc.*) comes to 173,855 days, 6 hours, 52 minutes, 44 seconds—or, to round it off—173,855 days. But, 69 "weeks"—483 years—is 173,880 days. This figure is 25 days short.

Jesus rode into Jerusalem on March 30, 33 AD. The starting point—Artaxerxes Longimanus' decree—was issued March 5. Add the missing 25 days and we come up with 173,880 days. *So, the prophecy predicted the event to the exact day!* This destroys the basis for the skeptic's argument, unless the forger was also divinely inspired. The point becomes moot. God was precise then, and He is equally accurate today!

FOUR WORLD EMPIRES

Daniel saw an image of four successive world empires. In order, he saw Babylon fall to the Media–Persian Empire, who fell to the Greek Empire, which fell to the Roman Empire. The prophet saw the destruction of each of the empires in detail—except Rome. From Daniel's perspective, Rome never ceases to exist, but is still in power on the day of the Lord! The prophet foresees the death of the Messiah, the destruction of Jerusalem and the Temple in AD 70, and in the same breath he identifies the coming Antichrist of the last days.

> **"After the sixty-two weeks the Messiah will be cut off and have nothing, and the people of the prince who is to come will destroy the city and the sanctuary."[22]**

"The people of the prince who is to come" did indeed destroy the city and the sanctuary. The Roman legions under the command of Titus sacked Jerusalem and destroyed the Temple. They, the Romans, are the people of the **"prince who is to come."** This coming prince is none other than the Antichrist, and according to this prophecy, he must come from the people and culture of ancient Rome.

ROME'S CONTINUING SPIRIT

Rome never actually fell; rather, it decayed from within. The Roman Empire waned in authority and power over the next 2,000 years, never regaining its

---

[22] Daniel 9:26.

former glory, but remnants of its authority and culture have remained on the scene.

MYSTERY ROME

The Roman Empire has gone through several incarnations. There was the political Rome of Jesus' day. As it declined, the spiritual Roman Empire of the Popes replaced it. They virtually ruled over the kings of Europe for the next 1,000 years. The era was befittingly called "the Dark Ages." During the Dark Ages, a European king could not hope to retain his kingdom unless he had the blessing of Rome. Anyone who claimed to be a Christian during those days also had to acknowledge the supremacy of the Pope, or face the Inquisition. The Roman Church burned tens of thousands of true Christians at the stake for refusing to accept that doctrine.

Following the Protestant Reformation, the authority of the Papacy waned in some parts of Europe, but not all. Both Charlemagne and Napoleon claimed their intent to restore the Holy Roman Empire as justification for their military conquests.

After Napoleon's defeat, the power of the Papacy declined. The Popes of Rome no longer dictate to kings, they retain their influence over populations. To this day, the "kings" of the earth still kneel in audience with the Pope. Even admitted atheist Mikhail Gorbachev knelt in the presence of Pope John Paul II in 1991. Papal pronouncements affect more than a billion Catholics worldwide.

It would be stretching a point to refer to Roman Catholicism as an "empire" in the secular sense of the word. But as a spiritual empire, it has no equal. It was as if the secular empire went "underground," so to speak—from the physical to the spiritual, physically dead, yet spiritually alive!

THE BIRTH PANGS OF AN EMPIRE

The carnage of World War II touched virtually every life on Planet Earth. Israel was reborn in the aftermath of the Holocaust. Without Hitler, Stalin would never have been able to develop his Eastern European hegemony. The war with Japan provided the impetus for the development of nuclear weapons. Often we forget the other victims of the Axis madness—the nations and peoples who lived under the heel of the Nazi political machine for years—even before the war was begun.

Nations like Holland, Belgium and tiny Luxembourg sought out alliances during the postwar reconstruction period. Two world wars in one century were enough. From the ashes of the Nazi occupation the Benelux alliance was born—in 1948! Holland, Luxembourg and Belgium formed the nucleus for the modern super state of Europe.

Modern Europe is an empire in every sense of the word, a single political entity, with the European Commission dictating political and economy policy to the largest single market on earth. The Benelux Treaty provided a war–weary population with another way to harness Europe's economic potential. As its success became apparent, the Benelux Customs Union attracted the attention of other European states. By 1957, three more nations—Italy, West Germany and Britain—joined under the Treaty of Rome to form the European Economic Community. By 1981, there were ten. By 1995, membership had grown to 15, and the modern European super state's growth potential appears unlimited.

Even the United States is interested. In 1991, James Baker, Secretary of State for George Bush called for a "new Atlanticism." He pointed out our "common European heritage" and the structure of NATO. The concept appeals to many European analysts. " 'In these circumstances,' says Colonel Andrew Duncan, assistant director of the International Institute for Strategic Studies in London, 'it is difficult to justify NATO on the scale it is today. What is needed is some sort of military–political organization based on NATO with both an American and a European pillar.' "[23]

The culture and people of the old Roman Empire permeate the territory of European hegemony today. A 17–member Commission of unelected political appointees who answer only to the European Commission president govern the European Community proper. The EC president owes his job to these unelected appointees. The Commission members are themselves carefully screened to ensure their primary loyalty is to the EC and not to their respective nations.

THE EIGHTH REICH

Europe has a six–month rotating presidency filled

[23] *TIME,* November 11, 1991, p. 64.

by the national leaders of the Community. But the real power rests with this handful of men who dictate policy from behind closed doors on the 13th floor of the EC's headquarters in Brussels. That political Roman Empire, Europe, was born in 1948. But, it has yet another incarnation. Ten nations out of the current EC will be taken over by the Antichrist as his power base. Seven will come willingly, and overthrowing its leaders will bring in three. From this power base, the Antichrist will bring the whole world under his control. This will be the eighth kingdom, and it will exist for seven years, during the Tribulation.

THE HARLOT AND THE BEAST

The Revived Roman Empire spoken of by Daniel the prophet receives greater attention by the Apostle John who describes it in the Book of the Revelation. In Revelation 17:3, 4 he describes his vision of this last–days government as an immoral woman, or harlot, sitting upon a beast. Specifically, John writes:

> "Then the angel carried me away in the Spirit into a desert. There I saw a woman sitting on a scarlet beast that was covered with blasphemous names and had seven heads and ten horns. The woman was dressed in purple and scarlet, and was glittering with gold, precious stones and pearls. She held a golden cup in her hand, filled with abominable things and the filth of her adulteries. This title was written on her forehead:

MYSTERY
BABYLON THE GREAT
THE MOTHER OF PROSTITUTES
AND OF THE ABOMINATIONS OF THE EARTH."[24]

Many things are often read into this and other passages that detail the composition of what will eventually be the government of the Antichrist. Many
have already done so in great detail. I will confine
ourselves to observations that can be documented.
For example, in December 1991, *TIME* Magazine ran
a series of articles on Europe's then–upcoming inte-
gration in January 1993. The Europlanners were facing an uphill battle as they attempted to convince the
various national populations that a borderless Europe
would be good for them.

> "Still, like patients bracing for an uncomfortable but
> ultimately beneficial treatment, West Europeans
> mostly welcome the plans for monetary and polit-
> ical union. Annual surveys by the EC show a
> steady rise in popular support for unification, with
> a solid majority favoring a common foreign and
> defense policy, a single currency and creation of a
> European central bank. 'Even uneducated workers
> understand,' says Louvain University public–opin-
> ion expert Jan Kerkhofs, 'that if Europe is not
> strengthened, Japan and the US will conquer more
> markets. People want a united Europe out of fear
> more than out of love.' Even though Project 1992
> is still incomplete, the EU now confronts more exis-
> tential questions about its future. Will there be a

[24] Revelation 17:3–5, NIV.

European currency and one central bank by 1997? Will the Twelve pledge themselves to achieve something like a United States of Europe in the not–too–distant future? As newly united Germany eagerly pushes forward and island Britain hangs back, the short–to–midterm outlook is for an artfully designed halfway house."[25]

John continues his prophecy about the resurrection of the old Roman Empire. He predicts: "**This calls for a mind with wisdom. The seven heads are seven hills on which the woman sits. They are also seven kings** [kingdoms]. **Five have fallen, one is, the other has not yet come; but when he does come, he must remain for a little while. The beast who once was, and now is not, is an eighth king** [kingdom]. **He** [It] **belongs to the seven and is going to his** [its] **destruction.**

"**The ten horns you saw are ten kings who have not yet received a kingdom, but who for one hour will receive authority as kings along with the beast. They have one purpose and will give their power and authority to the beast**" (Revelation 17:9–13 NIV).

The seven hills on which the woman sits refers to the literal geographical location of its capital, the seven ancient hills on which the city of Rome is founded. The city of Rome is positively identified in verse 18: "**The woman you saw is the great city that rules** [Greek, "is ruling"] **over the kings of the earth.**"

---

[25] *TIME,* December 9, 1991, *WORLD,* "Which Way to Maastricht, Mijnheer?" p. 39.

In John's day, only one city fit this description—Rome. So, Rome is the great whore known as Mystery Babylon the Great. Rome's religious system holds the key to its political resurrection.

The next verses describe the political kingdoms out of which this final form of gentile power ascended. John shows that he is giving another application of the symbol when he writes, **"They are ALSO seven kingdoms."** The five great empires that had fallen in his day are Egypt, Assyria, Babylon, Media–Persia and Greece. **"One is"** refers to Rome which followed Greece, and was in power in John's day. The one **"yet to come"** is the revived form of Rome, that will last a "short space"—about seven years, to be exact!

Rome, as a political system received a mortal wound, lingers in mystery form, and then revives to the astonishment of the world.

Ancient Rome was a political empire; and if we are to accept the prophecies of the Bible literally, then we should be looking for a genuine, political empire that will spring from the ruins of the Roman Empire of the ancients. The European Union has emerged from the old Roman culture. I believe the ten most powerful nations of this union will soon rise up and become the force behind the final resurrection of the Roman Empire, Phase 2—the last form of gentile power on earth. It will be destroyed by Jesus Himself. Its replacement will be the Kingdom of God, which will never be destroyed.

IMAGES ACROSS TIME...

A current interesting phenomena is the artwork used

by the Europlanners as part of their marketing strategy. For example, the second European commemo-
rative stamp depicts a woman riding on a beast. The
beast is pictured leaping across a body of water, and
swimming underneath it is a dolphinlike creature.
That is the image chosen for an official government
issued stamp.

> **"Then the angel said to me, 'The waters you saw,
> where the prostitute sits, are peoples, multitudes,
> nations and languages.' "**[26]

One Council of Europe public relations poster depicts
a partially rebuilt Tower of Babel with the slogan
"Europe: Many Tongues, One Voice." The imagery is
contagious. Within the *TIME* issue (December 1991),
page 13, the new Europe is symbolized as a scantily
dressed woman riding upon the back of a beast. She
is flying the European blue flag with a circle of gold
stars in the center. The woman in the picture is
accompanied by a multitude of people flying
European national flags. All are on the same beast.
Another picture in the same issue uses a graphic to
symbolize the obstacles the new Europe had yet to
overcome. Labeled "racism," "nationalism," "protec-
tionism," "tribalism" and "the legacy of communism," the graphic portrays these as a scarlet color,
like bloodstains, spreading across the back of the
beast. *TIME's* artist still shows the beast with a
woman riding upon its back. Compare these images,
some official government selections, and some
selected by a major global newsmagazine, to the

---

[26] Revelation 17:15 NIV.

image foreseen by John and recorded thousands of years before. Read all of Revelation Chapter 17. In particular, note verse 9:

> **"Here is the mind which has wisdom. The seven heads are seven mountains on which the woman sits...."**[27]

Many commentators have noted the fact that Rome is the "city on seven hills," generally in the context of the Roman Church. The Benelux Treaty of 1948 was the birth of the European Customs Union. Although it began the process, the political treaty that created the modern Europe was the 1957 Treaty of Rome!

Now consider this. One would assume that the public relations people whose primary goal is to present the emerging European super state as a positive development would use positive imagery. That is only logical.

If the Europlanners consciously selected Biblical imagery it is unlikely they would have chosen symbols so closely connected to the government of the Antichrist. In fact, the image selected as representative of Europe is of the Greek goddess Europa. Europe's chosen symbol is nothing less than Providential "coincidence." The dictionary contains this passage on Europa:

> "A Phoenician princess abducted to Crete by Zeus, who had assumed the form of a white bull, and by him the mother of Minos, Rhadamanthus, and Sarpedon."[28]

---

[27] Revelation 17:9 NASB.

[28] *The American Heritage Dictionary of the English Language,* Third Edition.

Interestingly, or perhaps ominously, Europa and the symbolism surrounding her was a favorite of Adolf Hitler, who often made reference to her in his speeches about the "Thousand Year Reich."

Europe's chosen symbol comes not from the Bible, but from pagan mythology. The Apostle John, peering across time, saw the images that the European planners selected to represent their new empire. He simply described what he saw from his 1st century perspective, and recorded it for the generation to which his description would be familiar. That generation would be the one Jesus spoke of as the one which would witness the reborn "fig tree."

COINCIDENCE OR FULFILLMENT?

It's time for a short review. The Bible says the government of the last days would have certain characteristics. It is to be global. It is to be forged, not through war, but through mutual agreement. The Bible uses the image of a woman riding on a beast as its identifying symbol. It must comprise the territory of the Old Roman Empire. Finally, it must emerge during the same generation as the rebirth of Israel. Although the Roman Empire is to revive as a peaceful alternative to military conquest, it must do so during a time of "wars and rumors of wars."

WHAT A COINCIDENCE!

The model for modern state of Europe was born in 1948—the same year as the rebirth of Israel. It was codified nine years later by what is known as the

Treaty of Rome. It came into being simultaneously with the emergence of the Cold War— the ultimate "rumor of war." Europe's own choice for a national symbol is a woman riding on a beast. If this were the only event predicted by the Bible to take place at the same time as the rebirth of a nation whose history was frozen in time for 2500 years, it would be astonishing.

But the Bible makes many other precise predictions. Each connects with the other, like building blocks. If this is the generation that Jesus spoke of, all of these predictions must happen in a single generation. All must be identifiable.

To make them unique, they must appear on the scene at the same time. They would have to develop at roughly the same speed. As we will see, the revival of the old Roman Empire is just one development that fits the Bible's timetable. There are hundreds more.

We face an "if–then" equation. If all these prophecies can be identified and documented as being fulfilled in one generation, then this generation must be the last before the Lord returns. If not, then the evidences documented here—and on the following pages—represent the most colossal coincidence in history. That conclusion would require a greater leap of faith than any necessary to accept the plain truth of Bible prophecy.

WHAT SHALL BE THE SIGN OF THY COMING?

The trends developing in our world today are simultaneously shocking, frightening, exhilarating, fascinating and disturbing. Who could have imagined microwave ovens, videocasette recorders and compact laser discs a generation ago? Not to mention gay rights, abortion rights, children's rights and even groups dedicated to protecting the rights of pedophiles. Children are taught evolution as fact instead of theory and that the Bible is a book of legends and fairy tales from which the myth of Creation was derived. One thing they are not taught: the events shaping our world were predicted, in detail, thousands of years ago, and recorded in the pages of that same Book—the Bible.

In Matthew's Gospel, Jesus was asked about the signs of His return at the end of the Church Age.

> **"And as He was sitting on the Mount of Olives, the disciples came to Him privately, saying, 'Tell us, when will these things be, and what will be the sign of Your coming, and of the end of the age?'"** [29]

His reply, referred to by scholars as the Olivet Discourse, is recorded, in various forms, in Matthew 24, Luke 21 and Mark Chapter 13. In it, He listed in detail the social, environmental, political and spiritual conditions that would prevail at that time. We'll explore these conditions—and the prophecies concerning them—in detail later in this book. These prophecies had to have a discernible trigger point. A road map is useless as a guide if you don't know where you started from or where you are now.

---

[29] Matthew 24:3.

CHAPTER 6
THE PARABLE OF THE FIG TREE

In Matthew 24:3 Jesus was really

asked two questions in one:

• When shall these things be?

• What will be the sign of Your coming

and of the end of the age?

He addressed Himself to question 2 for most of the chapter, before returning to question 1, "When shall these things be?" He told them:

> "Now learn the parable from the fig tree: when its branch has already become tender, and puts forth its leaves, you know that summer is near...."[30]

What does this mean? Many argue the "fig tree" refers to the restoration of Israel to her ancestral homeland. The fig tree is indeed a symbol for Israel today in much the same way the eagle symbolizes America or the bear is a symbol for Russia. But, if that were the entire story, identification of the fig tree as Israel would be pretty subjective. The Bible does refer to a fig tree some 33 times—18 times in the Old Testament alone. In context, the fig tree is always a symbol for Israel, such as Hosea's statement,

> "I found Israel like grapes in the wilderness; I saw your fathers as the earliest fruit on the fig tree in its first season."[31]

It is in that context that the symbolism of a blossoming fig tree in early spring is used. Just as that is a sure sign the general time of summer has arrived, so, the argument goes, is the restoration of Israel to her land a sure sign the general time of Christ's return has arrived. With that in mind, the verse following is stunning:

> "Truly I say to you, this generation will not pass away until all these things take place."[32]

---

[30] Matthew 24:32 NASB.

[31] Hosea 9:10 NASB.

[32] Matthew 24:34 NASB.

THIS GENERATION WILL NOT PASS???

One could expect something as important as **"the end of the age"** to be more clearly defined than a parable about a fig tree. After all, it was Jesus Christ who promised **"this generation will not pass."** Why didn't He just say, "The generation that sees the restoration of Israel to the land will not pass till all these things be fulfilled"? Why would He deliberately obscure an issue this important with vague references to trees, leaves and summertime?

But, it's important to recognize that the parable isn't just about Israel as the fig tree. Jesus said the leaves would symbolize:

- Religious deception and occult practices[33]
- Hot wars and Cold Wars (wars and rumors of wars)
- International revolution among nations
- Ethnic conflicts
- Famines
- Earthquakes
- Plagues[34]
- Global weather pattern changes
- Record killer storms

Like the first leaves on the fig tree, they would all come at the same time. Like birth pangs, they would all increase in frequency and intensity. And, the generation that saw all these things would not pass from the world stage until all of the prophecies of the last days—including His return—had come to pass.

---

[33] Matthew 24:4–7 (these verses cover points 1–6).

[34] Luke 21:25, 26 gives greater detail on points 7–9.

> "When these things *begin* [emphasis mine] **to take place, stand up and lift up your heads, because your redemption is drawing near.**"[35]

Keep in mind the audience to whom Jesus was speaking. The redemption He promised "would draw near" was the national redemption of Israel. He redeemed the Church (both Jew and Gentile who trusted in Him) at the Cross. That is an accomplished fact. Israel's national redemption in accordance with the Abrahamic covenant takes place at the Second Advent.

COULD IT BE ANY OTHER GENERATION?

The events of which He spoke could have applied to any generation in history—but could only be verified by looking backward.

Instead, His message was carefully addressed to one specific generation, somewhere in time, a generation to which His fig tree reference would make sense. That generation had to be able to identify the time in which it lived to the exclusion of all others. And Jesus defines a generation in a manner unique to Scripture. He says that the generation alive at the time of the rebirth of Israel will still be around at the Second Advent. Not 40 years, or three score and ten years, or even 120 years. He put it simply. If you were around in 1948, then, barring being hit by a bus, or run down by a runaway shopping cart, you can expect to be around to see all these things. All of them.

---

[35] Luke 21:28 NASB.

Understanding the times in which we live is not the exclusive domain of the theologian. Peter reminds us,

> **"But know this first of all, that no prophecy of Scripture is a matter of one's own interpretation."**[36]

The fact is, evidences pointing to this generation as *the* Generation are all around us, interconnected with such precision that no thinking person could honestly cry "Coincidence." A plan for human history, laid out in advance, with each detail recorded thousands of years in advance, can only come from God. Those details of Bible prophecy we will examine must all be fulfilled within one generation, and no other...or it is nothing more than "coincidence."

THE MOUNT OF OLIVES DISCOURSE

Now that we have established the existence and starting point of the global institutions that will serve as the Antichrist's springboard to global dictatorship, we will return to the prophecies of Matthew 24:7. Jesus spoke of much more than simply institutions created and developed by men for their use. I have no doubt that there are skeptics who will argue that such things were inevitable consequences of social advancement.

Jesus spoke of natural disasters. He said they would be linked to that generation in an identifiable way. To recap, the conversation began with a question:

---

[36] 2 Peter 1:20 NASB.

"And as He was sitting on the Mount of Olives, the disciples came to Him privately, saying, 'Tell us, when will these things be, and what will be the sign of Your coming, and of the end of the age?' " (Matthew 24:3).

It was a *private* conversation; one intended to be interpreted from the perspective of the questioners. The questioners were Jews, disciples of Jesus, yet they lived before the Church Age started. Their question was asked from Israel's perspective; and the answer clearly deals with what we all should recognize by now as the Tribulation period, when Israel will once again be GOD's central focus. That doesn't mean it has no bearing on the Church, anymore than discussing Russian politics has no bearing on the US. We watch Russian politics closely, to get some idea of how it will affect our world. But if we applied American political values to what is going on in Russia, we would get an inaccurate picture.

The signs given by Jesus for the last days have not been completely fulfilled. What we see happening all around us are the birth–pang signs all increasing in frequency and intensity, in concert with each other. This demonstrates to some degree how close the ultimate fulfillment these birth pangs are in relation to our present age. The fact is, the next firm event on the prophetic calendar is the Rapture of the Church. All the other signs that I have discussed thus far will not be completely fulfilled until after that takes place.

The unveiling of the Antichrist, the false prophet, the outbreak of the Gog–Magog War, the Mark of the

Beast, the signing of the seven–year covenant between Israel and her enemies—these cannot occur until after God removes His Church. However, we are seeing the increasingly heavy shadows of what is to come. Zola Levitt put it beautifully in a television broadcast. He said, "We are pushing at the membrane of time that separates the Church Age from the beginning of the Tribulation."

For the first time in history, we see a curious reversal in eschatological (the study of end time events) thinking. The Rapture could have taken place at any time in the last 2,000 years and still would have been right on schedule. But, now the Church serves as a sort of dam, holding back the events that are to come. So much of the groundwork is already laid that we are now in a sort of "holding pattern"—nothing is left to "set up." Now we wait for the return of Jesus Christ for the Church.

But that "set up" period—that's the exciting part! It began in earnest in 1948, slowly, almost imperceptibly, but it has reached a crescendo and threatens to engulf us...if the Lord tarries much longer. The political, social and economic stage is set; but what of the things exclusively beyond man's ability to influence or control?

ONLY GOD CAN MAKE A TREE

Jesus said this generation could be identified in direct proportion to its catastrophes, in both human and natural terms. He spoke of earthquakes, floods and unprecedented pestilence, or disease. Even insurance companies refer to such things as "acts of God"—and generally refuse to cover them without imposing a special premium.

Jesus also warned of wars and famines and ethnic unrest. Generally, these things are political in nature—but again, so far outside of human control, they rate a special exclusion in most insurance policies.

I mention insurance companies, not because they have some special "hot line" to God, or even because they don't. Insurers use a complicated system of actuarial tables—mathematical models that generally make it possible to predict what may or may not happen over a specific period of time to a specific portion of the population. That eliminates most of the risk, guaranteeing them a profit.

But earthquakes, wars, famines, civil unrest and disease are impossible to predict within a designated time frame with any margin of safety—unless, of course, you are God.

Jesus was not afraid to go where insurers fear to tread. He not only predicted these events, but also did so thousands of years in advance. He locked down the time to a single generation. Insurance actuarials are little more than odds makers; they calculate the odds of a person dying at a certain age by using the known facts—all people die—and the average age of death overall. They set their premiums according to the odds that the insured would exceed the average.

A BOOKIE'S NIGHTMARE

The odds against the predictions of all the events of

the Second Coming all coming to pass in a single generation—in any generation—are incalculable.

"H. Harold Hartzler, of the American Scientific Affiliation, writes in the foreword of Peter Stoner's book, 'the manuscript for *Science Speaks* has been carefully reviewed by a committee of the American Scientific Affiliation and by the Executive Council of the same group and has found, in general, to be dependable and accurate in regard to the scientific material presented. The mathematical analysis included is based upon principles of probability which are thoroughly sound and Professor Stoner has applied these principles in a proper and convincing way.' The following principles are taken from Peter Stoner in *Science Speaks* (Moody Press, 1963) to show that coincidence is ruled out by the science of probability. Stoner says that by using the modern science of probability in relation to eight prophecies, 'we find that the chance that any man might have lived down to the present time and fulfilled [all] eight prophecies is 1 in 10^{17}. [Stoner illustrates, supposing]...'we take 10^{17} silver dollars and lay them on the face of Texas. They will cover the entire state to a depth of two feet. Now mark just one of these silver dollars and stir the whole mass thoroughly, all over the state. Blindfold a man and tell him that he can travel as far as he wishes, but he must pick up the one marked silver dollar on the first try.' "[37]

Professor Stoner concludes the odds of it being the right silver dollar are 10^{17} and that was the equivalent odds

[37] *The Last Days of Planet Earth*, Jerry Johnston, Harvest House, 1991.

for eight prophecies made in advance, recorded and fulfilled in a single, future lifetime!

If we examined only the following, we could conclude fairly that Jesus beat all the odds.

> "And you will be hearing of wars and rumors of wars; see that you are not frightened, for those things must take place, but that is not yet the end. For nation will rise against nation, and kingdom against kingdom, and in various places there will be famines and earthquakes. But all these things are merely the beginning of birth pangs."[38]

"NATION SHALL RISE AGAINST NATION"

Scripture says, "**Examine everything carefully; hold fast to that which is good**" (1 Thessalonians 5:21), and when doing research it is sometimes helpful to examine the original words to clarify a meaning. To illustrate, imagine a future time—2,000 years from now—when some archeologist unearths a manuscript from our era and reads, "It is raining cats and dogs!" The statement, in vernacular, is accurate. It means it is raining very hard. But if our future archeologist failed to look into the common vernacular, he could well conclude that 2,000 years ago, cats and dogs fell from the sky!

What is rendered "**nation shall rise against nation**" in text is generally adequate to convey the meaning intended. But a closer examination show the Greek

---

[38] Matthew 24:6–8.

word translated "nation" is *ethnos*—the word from which we get the word *ethnic*. The word means "a race, or tribe"—not an inconsistent definition for our modern understanding of ethnicity.

It is also perfectly consistent in context, since what we understand today as being a **"nation"** was understood for centuries as a **"kingdom"** that is represented separately in the same verse.

So, by examining this verse in context, we find that one of the signs for the last days is that **"ethnic group shall rise against ethnic group"**—ethnic unrest!

There is no question that ethnic unrest is a problem of global proportions. There isn't a nation on earth untouched by some form of ethnic unrest. We usually think of it relative to color, like black and white, in the US, South Africa and other places. But Canada threatens to be ripped asunder by French vs. English. The former Yugoslavia is a powder keg of Serbs, Muslims, Croats and assorted combinations. That conflict even gave us the term "ethnic cleansing" as an alternative to the more common genocide.

Ethnicity is a factor throughout Africa—South Africa, Rwanda, Burundi, Somalia, Egypt, *etc*. Ethnicity is the key to understanding the Middle East. It is central to the internal problems of the Russian Federation. It plays a role in India, Pakistan, Bangladesh, Sri Lanka, Algeria, and France. I think you get the idea. It is a global problem. *TIME* Magazine reported in an October 9, 1995, article, "The Forgotten Wars," that there are some 46 ethnic wars raging around the world right now. But when and how did this explode into a global problem?

THE DEATH OF COLONIALISM

For most of the past 200 years, the major European powers invaded, subjugated and set up colonies in many places around the world. The legacies of colonialism are still apparent on the map. The Dutch Antilles, the US Virgin Islands, the British West Indies, and so on. It was colonialism that gave rise to the saying "the sun never sets on the British Empire." Before the Revolution, the United States was itself a colony of Great Britain.

At the close of World War II, the cost of maintaining colonial empires became too high for the colonial powers. The British had been bombed out of business; their only option available was to begin to divest it from foreign obligations. The former colonists themselves were tired of being ruled by dictators from foreign lands, and they were ready to take a hand at governing themselves. The same was true of the remaining colonies of Italy, France, the Netherlands and Portugal. It was just too expensive, and rapidly becoming politically incorrect.

The first domino to fall was the British colony of Burma. Sixty years of British oppression had not afforded the Burmese any protection against the Japanese, and they concluded the price was too high. In 1948, they declared their independence from Britain. The British were tired of their overseas occupation and were only too happy to see them go. Britain's reaction opened the floodgates.

THE "COINCIDENCES" OF 1948

It was 1948, more than any other single year, that shaped the geopolitical landscape we are currently facing. Israel's independence began a series of wars and conflicts between Arabs and Jews that are still unresolved.

In 1948, Kim Il Sung set up the Republic of North Korea, dividing the nation into North and South, resulting in a state of war between the two that exists to this day.

The French war of Indochina was a result of the French granting independence to Indochina in 1946. Two years later, the country divided into North and South Vietnam. That division between North and South set the stage for what became the longest and most costly political war in history. The US stepped into the conflict in the '60s and '70s. It changed the political landscape of that nation forever, bringing down a president, dividing a nation and forever changing the way Americans look at government.

The 1948 assassination of Indian leader Mahatma Gandhi was a pivotal event culminating in Indian independence the following year.

The gains made by Mao Tse Tung in 1948 forced the Chinese government to flee to Taiwan and gave birth to the People's Republic of China—a key player in the last days.

In 1948 Marshall Tito, recognizing Soviet inability to understand and control the ethnic dynamics at work in Yugoslavia, rebelled against Moscow's control of his nation. Yugoslavia was expelled from the Soviet Cominform. Freed from interference from Moscow, Tito was able to control his country's various ethnic factions from within. With his death, Yugoslavia splintered into ethnic conclaves like Bosnia, Serbia and Croatia.

As the various colonial empires were granted independence, a new spirit of ethnic pride was rekindled in nations who had lived for generations under a sort of "national schizophrenia." Countries previously held together by colonial powers splintered into smaller countries better suited to their ethnic makeup.

In 1948, the United Nations was composed of 66 nations. In the years following 1948, an additional 128 countries came into existence. These were not newly discovered countries that had been hidden on the other side of the planet. These were nations carved out of existing countries whose ethnic divisions were so profound that they could no longer coexist under the same roof, so to speak.

Now that we have Israel once again in the Land of Promise, the Bible says that certain other trends, unique to this generation, will begin to develop. A global economy will emerge to enable the Antichrist to fulfill his appointed destiny. The Book of the Revelation says that, at the peak of his power, the Antichrist will be so completely in control of the economy that even routine commerce will be under his thumb. Or more likely, at the mercy of his keyboard.

THE ULTIMATE WORK PERMIT

Revelation 13:17 says that no man will be able to buy or sell unless he is part of the Antichrist's economic system. Never in history was it possible for any one man to control all the buying and selling of a whole population, let alone a global population. Today, it's not only possible for all buying and selling to be controlled on a global basis, but we are seeing what can happen if only part of the system breaks down. In May 1998, a single satellite designated Galaxy 4 developed a little glitch in its software that caused it to fail to move into proper position at an appointed time. As a result, 90% of the pagers in America failed. Half the ATM's in the country went off line. Television and telecommunications failed. The month before, a little glitch in two of 145 AT&T frame relay switches shut down the nation's ATM network. During the outage, in excess of 5,000 corporations were unable to complete critical network-based business. Retailers were unable to authorize credit-card payments and financial institutions could not complete transactions. Engineers worked round the clock to locate the problem and fix it. Although initially only two frame relay switches failed, the cascade effect took over, and soon the entire network was down. What happened was a warning. First, it proves that it is entirely possible for a single individual—given the unquestionable authority to access the global computer network—to control all the buying and selling of every individual on earth. All that is necessary is to put everybody on earth into the electronic banking system. All that's needed is a bit of a push away from good old anonymous cash.

MANAGEMENT BY CRISIS

There is a bug in the global computer network. On January 1, 2000, computer systems will begin experiencing similar failures when mainframe computers will be unable to process dates. Here's a quick primer. In the early '60s, computer memory was at a premium, as was storage space. COBOL programmers hit on the idea of reducing storage space by only using the last two digits to represent years, using the MM/DD/YY formula. Computers would read December 31, 1999 as 12/31/99. Dates are replicated many times in programs, so by slashing the "19" off dates, it saved some $16 to $20 million per year over the last 30 years. Space is not so expensive now, but the programming remains. New programming was simply overlaid over existing COBOL programming, to make it compatible. Everyone thought eventually, somebody would develop a new basic system. But the COBOL one worked fine, and nobody ever did.

THE YEAR OF LIVING DANGEROUSLY

When the calendar rolls over to January 1, 2000, computers will read the date as 01/01/00—or, January 1, 1900. Unless it is fixed, every date dependent computer system in America will crash, freeze, or go haywire. Air traffic control computers won't be able to accept flight plans for flights, say, taking off on December 31 and landing January 1, because the computer will interpret the landing as occurring 100 years before takeoff. Traffic lights will fail. Banking transactions will spin out of control. Trains won't be able to move. The US rail system is 100% computer dependent. Computers tell the engineers when the tracks are clear. Nobody will know, so no trains will move. Without planes and trains, there will be no gas for automobiles or big trucks. Big cities will run out of food in days. Food riots are likely to occur shortly thereafter.

Even if planes don't fall from the sky and banks don't lose people's deposits, experts say we all will experience inconveniences from what is becoming widely recognized as the "year 2000 problem." They predict everything from disrupted travel schedules to more-serious problems, like large-scale power outages or even a global recession. The processing of tax refunds, veterans' benefits, and employee checks could be hampered, government auditors say. Indeed, in some places the problem is already upon us. One survey found that 44% of US companies had already experienced a year 2000 failure—like the grocery in Warren, Michigan, whose entire computer system crashed when a cashier tried to swipe a credit card bearing a 2000 expiration date.

Even the Pentagon's Global Command Control system—a key communication link during the Gulf War—failed a year 2000 readiness test last summer.

One risk–management executive describes a client he won't name—a Midwestern electric utility—that ran a test for Y2K compliance. When the test clock turned over to the year 2000, a safety system mistakenly detected dangerous operating conditions, and the power generators completely shut down. Programmers worked on the problem for three days, then reran the test. A different sector failed, shutting down the system again. Technicians have yet to fix the problem. The debacle underscored one of the most unsettling aspects of the Y2K bug: fixing the program that runs one piece of equipment can have disruptive effects on other parts of the system.[39]

CAN IT BE FIXED IN TIME?

One estimate is that it would take 80,000 COBOL programmers—starting now and working round the clock—just to keep Social Security checks flowing after the turn of the century. COBOL is a dead language. There aren't that many fluent, available COBOL programmers in the world. The Department of Defense won't be Y2K compliant until about 2019.

More than a year ago, Deputy Defense Secretary John Hamre decided to review how DoD's nuclear capability would be affected when the clock strikes January 1, 2000. The review comprises the command and control links US nuclear systems have with other domestic military systems and with other federal departments, like the Department of Energy and Department of State, as well as links with allied computer systems.

---

[39] *US News and World Report,* "Year 2000 Time Bomb," June 8, 1998.

"This is very important," Anthony Valletta, former assistant secretary of defense for command, control, communications and intelligence (C3I), said of the effort.

Valletta said the department is on track to take care of all its "mission critical" systems that have a Y2K glitch. The latter refers to the use by older computing languages of a two–digit code for the year date. Systems that use such code will malfunction on January 1, 2000, because they cannot correctly process the year 2000 date change.

"Military leaders of the United States, other NATO members and Russia must jointly assess the risk of an accidental nuclear missile launch or a provocative false alarm," according to a Y2K report last month by Edward Yardeni, chief economist for Deutsche Morgan Grenfell Inc.[40]

The DoD is downsizing personnel and upgrading computer weapons systems, using satellite Global Positioning System technology. Just to operate now, it requires 200,000 software professionals. The systems will shut down January 1, 2000, leaving the US blind and defenseless.

Experts are taking the crisis seriously, while the government is pretending everything will be just fine. Maybe it will be, for America, who knows? But America is one country among many. And fixing computer programs is only part of the solution.

[40] "Dod Focuses on Preventing Nuclear Chaos" from Y2k C4I NEWS, Vol. 5, No. 34, May 21, 1998.

FIXING CHIPS IS LIKE FIXING YOUR DNA

Even if they do, however, another problem looms: embedded chips. Unlike software, the microchips running everything from nuclear power plants to off-shore oil rigs cannot simply be rewritten. Like the chip inside your VCR or microwave, these devices are not accessible. The commands are physically burned onto the chip. The only way to update a non–compliant power plant or robot–filled automobile factory floor is to determine which chips will malfunction and then replace each one individually. In the case of an offshore refinery, it means sending divers hundreds of feet under the ocean surface.

In a recent interview with the Reuters news agency, the Central Intelligence Agency accepted the fact that there will be numerous failures of such systems around the world. But instead of focusing on the technological side of the crisis, the CIA is already collecting data on what their "Y2K" chief calls the "social, political and economic tumult" that could result. That is, the agency is evaluating individual societies to determine how disruptions in electric power, banking, and other essential services might affect them.

EVEN "FOGGYBOTTOM" IS NERVOUS

The CIA predicts that newly developed nations, like those in Asia and Latin America, will be the hardest hit. While the US, Britain, and Australia have had enough time to head off the worst disruptions, as well as a fairly stable social fabric, many other nations who only recently adopted computer technology do not now have the money to invest in diagnosing all their systems, nor the political climate to ensure public safety.[41]

It would take 300,000 COBOL programmers full time to avert that. Same problem. Telephones, TV satellites—the whole global communications network is computer dependent. What do you think will happen when nobody can communicate? In one day, we'll be moved back 100 years, technologically. How will that affect the stock market? Is such a catastrophe sufficient to be the vehicle upon which the Antichrist will rise to prominence?

WHO IS LIKE UNTO THE BEAST?

Apparently, all our hopes are pinned on developing a "magic bullet" program that will fix the Y2K problem. That's about as likely as developing a single pill that will cure AIDS and all AIDS–related ailments like TB, cancer, Kaposi's sarcoma, *etc.* Not very likely, without a little extra help.

JUST SUPPOSE

The Antichrist, energized and indwelt by Satan, may well come up with that magic bullet. Having fixed the problem, it takes no stretch of the imagination to assume he will suddenly be propelled to the forefront of the electronic commerce debate. Having brought the world back from the brink of electronic

---

[41] *The Guardian*, May 21, 1998, Douglas Rushkoff.

catastrophe, using technology he alone developed, would it not make sense to give him the authority to ensure such a danger never threatens the world's financial markets again? In fact, given the threat the Millennium Bug poses to the global electronic defense systems, one wouldn't have to stretch too far to see him taking over control of the mission critical computers for the various world defense systems as well.

In July 1996, President Clinton signed Executive Order 13010. It created the President's Commission for Critical Infrastructure Protection (PCCIP) which was designed to allow the federal government to "protect continuity of government" from acts of terrorism, both physical and electronic.

That means telecommunications, electrical power systems, gas and oil storage and transportation, banking and finance systems, transportation capability, water supply systems, emergency services (medical, police, and fire department.) are all under PCCIP. Although this commission's charter does not mention Y2K–caused breakdowns, on Feb. 4, 1998, President Clinton signed an Executive Order to establish a commission to protect the very same infrastructure segments from Y2K failure.

The 104th Congress has passed a variety of measures that will be very effective in the hands of a global megalomaniac like the Antichrist. Here are just a few:
- A national database of all employed people.
- One hundred pages of new "health care crimes," for which the penalty is (among other things) seizure of assets from both doctors and patients.

- The largest gun confiscation act in US history—which also is an unconstitutional ex–postfacto law, and the first law ever to remove people's constitutional rights for the committing of a misdemeanor.
- A law banning guns in ill–defined school zones; random roadblocks may be used for enforcement; gun bearing residents could become federal criminals for just stepping outside their doors or getting into vehicles.
- Increased funding for the Bureau of Alcohol, Tobacco and Firearms, an agency infamous for its ineptitude.
- A law enabling the Executive Branch to declare various groups "terrorist" without stating any reason, and without the possibility of appeal. Once a group has been so declared, its mailing and membership lists must be turned over to the government.
- A law authorizing secret trials with secret evidence for certain classes of people.
- A law requiring that all states begin issuing drivers licenses carrying Social Security numbers and "security features" (such as magnetically coded fingerprints and personal records) by October 1, 2000. By October 1, 2006, "neither the Social Security Administration, or the Passport Office, or any other federal agency, or any state or local government agency may accept for any evidentiary purpose a state driver's license or identification document in a form other than one issued with a verified Social Security number and 'security features.' "
- A law creating a national database, now being constructed, that will contain every exchange and

observation that takes place in your doctor's office. This includes records of everything from prescriptions to private conversations with your doctor. It also includes by law, any statements you and any observations your doctor makes about your mental or physical condition, whether accurate or not, whether made with your knowledge or not.

These new congressional laws are not aimed at a Y2K crisis, but they will certainly be invoked if such a crisis develops. With the coming of Y2K we can also expect the use of the "Expedited Funds Availability Act of 1987," which will restrict bank withdrawals (of cash) through several mechanisms. There are also dozens of laws from the "War on Drugs" that prohibits citizens from withdrawing their legally earned money from their own accounts, except with government notification. And don't forget, the "War Powers Act of 1917" is still on the books. Under its "Trading with the Enemy" provisions, which President Roosevelt expanded in 1933 to include US citizens as enemies, citizens' gold and currency can be confiscated and manipulated to the government's benefit.

With laws like the above, the Y2K collapse does not have to be severe to result in severe government actions.

LEST WE DESTROY OURSELVES FROM THE FACE OF THE EARTH

During the Iraqi standoff in February 1998, the Pentagon's computer network came under an intense three–week electronic bombardment. Senior

Pentagon officials reported to the White House that an Iraqi electronic attack was underway against the Defense Department's computer network. At least 11 Pentagon computer network sites were hit. Other sites were probably also breached. The Pentagon traced the attackers around the world several times but could not find the source. Several of the attacks passed through the United Arab Emirates, while others were traced to Germany and Israel. The official said the timing of the attacks prompted "a very large amount of concern at the high levels of the Department of Defense." The situation was so severe Pentagon officials declared a DEFCON 1 alert. The US even began planning a response to the Iraqi electronic attack. Finally, the FBI was able to track down the info warriors. The culprits were two high school students in Cloverdale, California, and a young Israeli computer whiz.

The need for a super systems security expert is undeniable.

The Biblical system of the Beast will certainly give rise to the Beast incarnate. He'll have answers, not just in cyberspace, but for the seemingly intractable political problems across the globe.

STAGE THREE

CHAPTER 7

THE RAPTURE FACTOR

One of the most compelling—and most often

misunderstood—events still pending, according

to Bible prophecy, is an event called the Rapture

of the Church. Simply stated, it is the time when

the last believer has been called and Jesus Christ

issues a great shout: "Come up here."

At that moment, the graves containing every believer who has ever died since Pentecost will open. The molecules of every one of those believers will be reconstituted. In a moment, in the twinkling of an eye, they will be raised, in perfect, immortal bodies. Those bodies will ascend into the air where they will be met by Jesus Christ, their Redeemer. The believers who are still alive will vanish immediately thereafter, and will ascend with them to meet the Lord in the air. The Bible says it this way:

> "But we do not want you to be uninformed, brethren, about those who are asleep, that you may not grieve, as do the rest who have no hope. For if we believe that Jesus died and rose again, even so God will bring with Him those who have fallen asleep in Jesus. For this we say to you by the word of the Lord, that we who are alive, and remain until the coming of the Lord, shall not precede those who have fallen asleep. For the Lord Himself will descend from heaven with a shout, with the voice of the archangel, and with the trumpet of God; and the dead in Christ shall rise first. Then we who are alive and remain shall be caught up together with them in the clouds to meet the Lord in the air, and thus we shall always be with the Lord. Therefore comfort one another with these words."[42]

Skeptics are fond of pointing out that the word "Rapture" does not appear in the Bible. Well, the word "Bible" doesn't appear in the Bible, either. The

---

[42] 1 Thessalonians 4:13–18 NASB.

word "rapture" comes from the Latin word *rapios,* which means, literally, to be "caught up" or "snatched away." Rapios is translated into Latin from the Greek word *harpazo* (ἁρπάζω) which means "to seize, or to carry off by force." The word was generally used to describe a pickpocket. Clearly, in context, the idea of a Rapture is one of being suddenly, instantly transfigured and carried away. Precisely as 1 Thessalonians 4:13–18 says in clear, unmistakable terms.

The Rapture is a signless event. That means that it comes without warning. It could have occurred in the days of the Apostle Paul, it could have occurred in the days of Henry the VIII, and it would neither have been early or late. That is known as the doctrine of imminence. Don't be fooled by people who tell you they have calculated the date. It's not only impossible, it is knowledge forbidden to men and known only to God.

> "But of that day and hour no one knows, not even the angels of heaven, nor the Son, but the Father alone. For the coming of the Son of Man will be just like the days of Noah. For as in those days which were before the flood they were eating and drinking, they were marrying and giving in marriage, until the day that Noah entered the ark, and they did not understand until the flood came and took them all away; so shall the coming of the Son of Man be."[43]

---

[43] Matthew 24:36–39 NASB.

THE CALL

The Book of the Revelation discusses the concept of a secret Rapture a little further. The first three chapters of the Book of the Revelation deal with the seven Churches and correspond to seven particular epochs, or ages within the Church Age itself. We'll discuss each of these in more detail as we progress. The Book of the Revelation itself is written in chronological order, so, as the Church Age draws to a close in Chapter 3, Chapter 4 begins with a shout.

> **"After these things I looked, and behold, a door standing open in heaven, and the first voice which I had heard, like the sound of a trumpet speaking with me, said, 'Come up here, and I will show you what must take place after these things.'"**[44]

That shout *"Come up here"* is the Rapture of the Church. From that moment forward in the Book of the Revelation, never again is the Church mentioned as being an earthly institution.

WHAT HAPPENS NEXT?

All the believers who have been raptured, or snatched away, will meet the Lord, face to face, in the air. In addition, all the believers who have been parted by death will once again be in the physical presence of their loved ones, never to be separated again. We will recognize one another, and the joy we'll experience is nothing short of heavenly (no pun

---

[44] Revelation 4:1 NASB.

intended). The Bible says that the unsaved dead remain in their graves until the Great White Throne Judgment. But for those who find themselves in the air with the Lord, three things happen.

First, there is a glorious meeting with the Lord and with all our loved ones who have departed before us.

Secondly, there is the Bema Seat of Christ. That is also called the "Believers' Judgment." Each of us will stand before Christ and give account of ourselves for those things we have done in the body during our lifetime. This is different than the Great White Throne Judgment, which takes place at the end of the Millennium. The Great White Throne is the Judgment Seat of unbelievers. At the Great White Throne Judgment, everyone who ever lived and died without Christ will also be resurrected to judgment. Because the unbeliever rejected Christ as his Advocate, that judgment will be the one that all deserve—the Lake of Fire for eternity. The Bible calls that the "second death."

> "Be faithful until death, and I will give you the crown of life. 'He who has an ear, let him hear what the Spirit says to the churches. He who overcomes shall not be hurt by the second death.' "[45]

The Bema Seat takes its name using imagery from Paul's day. During the ancient Olympics, the judge sat along the finish line. His purpose was not to

---

[45] Revelation 2:10, 11 NASB.

determine whether or not the participants actually ran the race. If they got that far, then they completed the course. But the Judge at the Bema seat determined how they came in—first, second, and so on, and he handed out the rewards. That is the imagery that the Bible gives us of Believer's Judgment. It is at the Judgment Seat of Life that Christ metes out the rewards—not the punishments that we earn in life. The punishments He has already dealt with by shedding His Blood on the Cross for all those who were willing to trust in Him. Your rewards are determined according to your works. That is the only place in which your works have any bearing on your eternity. Works won't save you. Only faith in Christ's completed Work on your behalf will. But your works do have a bearing as to your rewards.

> **"But let each man be careful how he builds upon it. For no man can lay a foundation other than the one which is laid, which is Jesus Christ. Now if any man builds upon the foundation with gold, silver, precious stones, wood, hay, straw, each man's work will become evident; for the day will show it, because it is to be revealed with fire; and the fire itself will test the quality of each man's work. If any man's work which he has built upon it remains, he shall receive a reward. If any man's work is burned up, he shall suffer loss; but he himself shall be saved, yet so as through fire."[46]**

---

[46] 1 Corinthians 3:10b–15 NASB.

Your gold, silver and precious stones are works done with the right motive—and by dependence upon the power of the Holy Spirit.

THE MARRIAGE SUPPER OF THE LAMB

Following the distribution of rewards at the Judgment Seat of Christ, there's a big party—and we are all invited! The Bible calls this the Marriage Supper of the Lamb. On earth, the human race is about to undergo the 21 Judgments of God against a sinful and unrepentant human race. But we will be guests at the mother of all parties. Jesus painted a word picture of that event by using the tradition of the day. When a man sought a bride, he would first go to the father and offer a sum to purchase the bride. That was called the dowry. Following that, he would leave to build a dwelling place for his new wife. When it was completed, the bride's father would inspect it to make sure it was worthy of his daughter. Finally, when all was said and done, the bridegroom would arrive at his bride's house in secret, where he would sweep her off her feet and carry her to their new honeymoon cottage. The happy couple would then stay in seclusion in their new home for seven days. Jesus paid the price of His Bride—the Church—with His own Blood, shed at Calvary. The Bible says He then began construction of our eternal home.

> "Let not your heart be troubled; believe in God, believe also in Me. In My Father's house are many dwelling places; if it were not so, I would have told you; for I go to prepare a place for

you. And if I go and prepare a place for you, I will come again, and receive you to Myself; that where I am, there you may be also."[47]

Having prepared a place for us, we can be certain of the remainder of His promise. He will come again, and He will receive us to Himself, that where He is, there we will be also! What a tremendous promise!

PEAKS IN TIME

In Chapter Five, we discussed the 69 weeks of Daniel. Remember, he foresaw a period of 70 weeks of years in Israel's future history. After 69 weeks, Daniel writes, the Messiah will be killed. Then, Daniel's prophecy goes into hibernation. Years go by, and yet there is still one unfulfilled week determined or allotted to Daniel's people (the Jews) and the holy city (Jerusalem). Shortly after the Rapture, the time clock resumes its countdown.

The Bible often refers to the Church as a mystery. In God's economy, a mystery is not a whodunit novel, but rather an event not previously revealed by God. So when Daniel was given his vision, he saw it from beginning to end, without that parenthetical period that was occupied by the Church. Think of it this way. Imagine a man standing behind a mountain. Way off in the distance, he sees a second mountain peak. What he can't see is the valley between the two peaks. That is the way Old Testament prophets saw the unfolding of history. Daniel saw the peak upon which the Lord was crucified, and he saw the peak in

---

[47] John 14:1, 2.

time in which the Lord returns. In the middle was the mystery Church. With the Church out of the way, Daniel's vision resumes.

TARRY UNTIL I COME

When Jesus explained His upcoming betrayal and death, Peter asked Him who the betrayer was. Not getting an answer, he began ticking off the names of possible candidates.

> **"Peter, turning around, saw the disciple whom Jesus loved following them; the one who also had leaned back on His breast at the supper, and said, 'Lord, who is the one who betrays You?' Peter therefore seeing him said to Jesus, 'Lord, and what about this man?' Jesus said to him, 'If I want him to remain until I come, what is that to you? You follow Me!' This saying therefore went out among the brethren that that disciple would not die; yet Jesus did not say to him that he would not die, but only, 'If I want him to remain until I come, what is that to you?' "[48]**

The Book of the Revelation records that John did indeed 'tarry' until Jesus came to him. While in exile on the Island of Patmos off the coast of Greece, an old man was suddenly startled by a vision. He saw the glorified Jesus, who had a message for a future generation, somewhere in time, and details about the missing 70th Week of Daniel. John opens his

[48] John 21:20–23.

Book with these words, making clear the Divine chain of authorship and the transmission of the message. John also bore eyewitness to the Author, whom John knew personally during His earthly ministry.

> "The Revelation of Jesus Christ, which God gave Him to show to His bond–servants, the things which must shortly take place; and He sent and communicated it by His angel to His bond–servant John, who bore witness to the word of God and to the testimony of Jesus Christ, even to all that he saw. Blessed is he who reads and those who hear the words of the prophecy, and heed the things which are written in it; for the time is near."[49]

Note the elements contained in these first three verses. First, it is the Revelation of Jesus Christ. Secondly, Jesus was given the Commission to reveal it to John by God the Father. Third, these were addressed to His bond–servants, the Church. Fourth, they were communicated to John, an eyewitness to Jesus' earthly ministry who did indeed tarry for this purpose. As we have already discussed, the Book of the Revelation is laid out in chronological order. The first three chapters deal with the seven churches in Asia Minor at that time. Each of those churches corresponded with a then future epoch, or period of time within the Church Age. The last of these churches to be addressed is the church of Laodicea. That is the current Church period, and the Lord doesn't have much good to say about it.

---

[49] Revelation 1:1–3.

"And to the angel of the church in Laodicea write:

The Amen, the faithful and true Witness, the Beginning of the creation of God, says this: 'I know your deeds, that you are neither cold nor hot; I would that you were cold or hot. So because you are lukewarm, and neither hot nor cold, I will spit you out of My mouth. Because you say, "I am rich, and have become wealthy, and have need of nothing," and you do not know that you are wretched and miserable and poor and blind and naked, I advise you to buy from Me gold refined by fire, that you may become rich, and white garments, that you may clothe yourself, and that the shame of your nakedness may not be revealed; and eye salve to anoint your eyes, that you may see. Those whom I love, I reprove and discipline; be zealous therefore, and repent. Behold, I stand at the door and knock; if anyone hears My voice and opens the door, I will come in to him, and will dine with him, and he with Me."[50]

It is out of this church, "wretched and miserable and poor and blind and naked," that the Lord calls His Bride home, before she could defile herself further, proving the love of God does indeed surpass all understanding!

LEFT BEHIND

But from the perspective of those left behind, pande-monium reigns supreme. To all intents and purposes,

---

[50] Revelation 3:16 NASB.

millions of people have simply vanished. Where a man had stood one second ago, only his clothes remain.

Just picture the scene:

John had a terrible day. Nothing went right. "One more time," his foreman warned him. "The next time you come in here hung over and unable to run this machine properly, and you're outta here. There's plenty of guys with lunch pails lined up just waiting for your job." *Yeah, right,* John thought, as he made the familiar corner two blocks from his house. *Who else would they get to stand there and punch a button, remove the part, put in another piece of molding, punch a button, remove a part...and all that for half the money that I'm worth?* As he daydreamed about the day when he could tell his foreman to take his job and... *Wait a minute! Is that guy crazy?* He looked up to see a bus barreling down the road on his side. John swerved crazily, jumping the curb and going directly into someone's yard. The bus hit the tree out front that John narrowly missed. He jumped out of his car and stormed to the bus, half hoping the driver had killed himself, and half hoping there'd be enough of him left for John to punch out. He boarded the bus through the door that had been sprung by the collision. "Where's the driver?" he demanded, angrily. Inside the bus people were screaming, but there was something odd about the whole thing. For one thing, there was no driver. And the people on the bus weren't screaming in pain, or even fear. It was something else. A woman cried;

"Where are my teenagers? They were both here just a minute ago." A middle–aged man was frantically searching under seats for his wife. All he found were her clothes. John left the bus in a hurry. *What in the world is happening?* he thought. He looked up the street, and there were collisions all over the neighborhood. People were screaming out the names of husbands, wives, children, friends, as cars careened insanely in the streets. John abandoned any thought of punching out the bus driver. Instead, he began to walk, then to jog, and finally, broke out into a full gallop toward his own house two blocks away. As he watched in horror, a helicopter simply fell to the ground on Dunn Street, just a block parallel to his house. Spinning out of control, it took the top off the old elm tree, its rotor catching in the branches, causing it to rotate once around the tree before being slung like a stone from a slingshot into Rick's garage next door. It burst into flames on impact. John reached his front door, leaping over a US Postal Service uniform lying in a heap on his front doorstep. He ran into his house, calling—no screaming, his wife's name. "Fran! Fran, where are you?" He found her in the living room, transfixed before the television set. CNN had just broken in with a special report. He listened. "Ladies and gentlemen, this is a special report. I... I don't quite know where to begin this story. Moments ago, reports starting coming into our news room of people vanishing into thin air. The highways are clogged with driverless cars, aircraft pilots have disappeared from their controls. There seems to be no rhyme or reason to it. Men, women, children, babies have just disappeared. But not everybody, obviously. The disappearances cut across all walks of life. In particular, it seems, young babies constitute the only group that have not seen at least a few spared. Even some of the technicians in our own news room simply vanished. We'll have more on this breaking news story as it develops, as soon as we can locate some people to operate our camera equipment. In the meantime, stay indoors, lock your doors, and stay tuned. We'll be the first with the story, as it happens." The anchor droned on and on, repeating the same sentences with slight variations as he tried to make sense of the information at hand. But John had tuned him out in his mind. "Thank God, Fran, you're still here." He went to the fridge and opened a beer. Then, with a start, he turned to her. "What about our son? Have you heard anything?" Fran was silent, in shock. Then she shook herself free of the paralysis that had gripped her. "It's OK. Jimmy came home from high school a few minutes ago. He's in the basement with one of his friends. John raced down the stairs. Jimmy was there, crying. He looked up and said, "Dad, I didn't do anything. I was just sitting here talking with Tommy and he just... he just..." Jimmy pointed to the pile of clothes in the chair opposite him.

WHERE IS EVERYBODY?

As you can well imagine, there will be considerable confusion following the Rapture of the Church, and it won't be confined to individual neighborhoods. Entire governments will be decimated as the best and the brightest join the Lord in the air. Those left behind will have to fend for themselves, without any moral compass to guide them. Nations will blame each other for using some secret weapon against them. Others will point out the predictions of Nostradamus, or find some sense in the argument that aliens came and took everybody way. There are certain New Age groups who have long held to the belief of a quantum leap in spiritual evolution. Here is an excerpt from one of the many New Age "explanations" for an event that defies explanation, apart from God.

THE FUTURE ACCORDING TO THE NEW AGE

- "Expect much change to society, weather, yourself. This need not be negative, but exciting, leading to a new Galactic civilization by the year 2012.

- "Time will seem to speed up (the Mayan calendar says we are moving beyond time and money).

- "There will be an official announcement of contact with extraterrestrials in 1997–1998— probably from the US Government.

- "Earthquakes, eruptions will probably increase, but there will not be a massive rise in the water level. This is 'Mother Earth' cleansing herself.

- "There will be much jockeying for power over the next few years between the military, the secret government / New World Order / Illuminati / Vatican and some extraterrestrials.

- "The banking system will probably collapse (the Mayan calendar says we are going beyond time and money).

- "The New World Order will attempt to be in power by 2003. This will probably be short lived. We may wake one day to the headline that the banking system has collapsed, we each have $500 of credits– units in a central system and we must use a Smartcard for all transactions.

- "President Clinton will probably be the last elected US president. He will not complete his term.

- "There is a possibility of a fake Second Coming (the return of Jesus Christ) staged by the negative Grey extraterrestrial. This could be an aerial hologram. This could be staged to divide us and distract us. The Second Coming is really within us.

- "Some people will be 'checking out' due to their inability to handle the new higher spiritual frequencies or energies coming to our planet. This will be their choice. [Note, this is a blatant false prophecy designed to explain away the Rapture of the true Church.]

- "Expect newly born children to be intelligent, highly intuitive and spiritual leaders.

- "Use of the Mayan Calendar will become more widespread. It is a natural cycle calendar that stimulates synchronicity and telepathy. Use of the calendar in everyday life will help heal the planet, break the vicious link between time and money and bring oneness and understanding to humanity."[51]

COUNTERFEITING BIBLE PROPHECY

Note how close some of this drivel is to Bible prophecy. It was Hitler who said "the best lie contains just enough truth to make it palatable." Our New Agers mention earthquakes and volcanic eruptions, but no flood. That's what the Bible says—but it isn't "Mother Nature" cleansing herself. It's a fulfillment of a promise made to Noah and further expanded on by Jesus Himself. The New World Order is a definite likelihood, but not for the reasons the New Agers think. The Bible promises a world government under the Antichrist. We'll go into that in greater detail later.

The same is true for the banking collapse and the creation of electronic money—a direct fulfillment of Revelation 13:17, which says that no man will be able to buy or sell unless he has a mark that signifies

---

[51] *2012 Unlimited*, New Age Internet Group, June 2, 1998.

he is a member in good standing of the Antichrist's New World Order. Such an event was never possible prior to the development of computers, and control of all buying and selling would, by definition, require an electronic commerce system.

And then, of course, the possibility of a "fake" Second Coming of Jesus Christ. That would explain to those left behind where everybody else went. They "faked" a Second Coming, probably with the assistance of the aliens that our New Age friends are so sure we'll encounter. Also, notice that in the New Age view, this "checking out" will be voluntary. It will seem like it at first. Later on in the Tribulation, plenty of people will be "checking out," and it will be voluntary. Those "checking out" will choose to do so rather than submit to the government of the beast and his mark. When they "check out," it will be in two parts: one part is the body; the other part will be the head. They will depart separately as the penalty for refusing the mark of the beast. We'll go into this in greater detail, also.

GREAT LIES REQUIRE A GREATER LIAR

It is into this atmosphere that one will appear, having a look more stout than his fellows, and speaking great things. He'll have answers to the questions that currently plague the globe, including the one that will explain where everybody went. The Bible describes him—and his modus operandi this way:

> "And then that lawless one will be revealed whom the Lord will slay with the breath of His

mouth and bring to an end by the appearance of His coming; that is, the one whose coming is in accord with the activity of Satan, with all power and signs and false wonders, and with all the deception of wickedness for those who perish, because they did not receive the love of the truth so as to be saved. And for this reason God will send upon them a deluding influence so that they might believe what is false, in order that they all may be judged who did not believe the truth, but took pleasure in wickedness."[52]

[52] 2 Thessalonians 2:8–12 NASB.

CHAPTER 8
A WORLD WITHOUT RESTRAINT

During the Church Age, the Holy Spirit of God

personally indwelt all believers. His ministry acted

as the restraining influence against evil. It is through

the Holy Spirit that the Bible functions as the living,

breathing Word of God. The Holy Spirit is the One

who protects the true Church against delusion

and false teaching. But the Bible teaches that His

ministry undergoes a fundamental change once

the Church has been removed from the earth.

When Paul wrote his Epistle to the Thessalonians, he addressed a heretical notion that was already being circulated by a forged letter to the Thessalonians. It taught that the Rapture had already taken place, and that the Thessalonians had been left behind. Paul explains in detail the order of events, beginning with 2 Thessalonians 2:1 and following.

> **"Now we request you, brethren, with regard to the coming of our Lord Jesus Christ, and our gathering together to Him, that you may not be quickly shaken from your composure or be disturbed either by a spirit or a message or a letter as if from us, to the effect that the day of the Lord has come."**

Paul explained that there were certain events that would precede the introduction of the Antichrist. In particular, he warned that before the Antichrist could come on the scene, there would first have to be a great apostasy. The word *apostasy* comes from the Greek word ἀποσασία (apostasia) which means, literally, "to defect, or to forsake the faith."

> **"Let no one in any way deceive you, for it will not come unless the apostasy comes first, and the man of lawlessness is revealed."**[53]

In this generation, we have set the standard for apostasy. There have always been heretical views, of course, just as there have always been earthquakes, famines and wars. But this generation has elevated it to an art form.

---

[53] 2 Thessalonians 2:3 NASB.

IF EVERYBODY IS GOD, THEN WHO IS GOD, REALLY?

The blending together of Christianity, the New Age, Eastern religions, pantheism and mysticism has created a single, eclectic spiritual gumbo, so to speak. And this blend creates a theology without God. Man is God, God is man, and all kinds of other non-sense—but wrapped in Christian sounding themes, with a kind of christ thrown in for seasoning. A perfect Satanic counterfeit! The Bible says God created man in His own image. In Satan's mirror image religion, man creates God in man's image. When that happens, we have a mess that generally fits into the category of New Age.

Just the other day, I was shopping in a Barnes & Noble bookstore. The section marked "Religion" held one shelf of Bibles and other Christian materials. The same section devoted the remaining eight shelves to various New Age, Hindu, Buddhist or other Eastern religions. Fifty years ago, one would have to find a specialty store to locate even a single book of Buddhism. Today, finding a Bible in a secular book store is a rarity. It is into an atmosphere of apostasy after the restraining influence of the Holy Spirit is removed (the Church) that the Antichrist is revealed:

> "and the man of lawlessness is revealed, the son
> of destruction, who opposes and exalts himself
> above every so–called god or object of worship,
> so that he takes his seat in the temple of God,
> displaying himself as being God. Do you not

remember that while I was still with you, I was telling you these things? And you know what restrains him now, so that in his time he may be revealed."[54]

HIS TIME IS COMING

Once the Church is gone, Satan's counterfeit Christ is allowed to make his appearance. Second Thessalonians 2:11 says that the man of sin comes **"in accord with the activity of Satan, with all power and signs and false wonders."** According to Revelation 13, one of those false wonders is the healing, or apparent healing, of a mortal head wound.

> **"And I saw one of his heads as if it had been slain, and his fatal wound was healed. And the whole earth was amazed and followed after the beast...."**

There will be some Satanic counterfeit "miracle" whereby the Antichrist is apparently raised from the dead. John merely says that the wound that he saw was "as if" it had been slain. There is no question that from this point on, the beast is Satanically energized—and the world, deprived of the Holy Spirit's influence, buys into it, hook, line and sinker. It is human nature to seek out something or someone supernatural to worship. God built us that way. Without God, the world will only have secular humanism (the worship of humanity as the supreme being)—and that isn't very satisfying. Despite claims to the contrary from Psychic Hotline, it's pretty obvious

---

[54] 2 Thessalonians 2:3–6 NASB.

that we're not supreme. Satan, on the other hand, will offer a world without God somebody to worship. John says that humanity will jump at the chance:

> **"and they worshiped the dragon, because he gave his authority to the beast; and they worshiped the beast, saying, 'Who is like the beast, and who is able to wage war with him?' "[55]**

It's not like this is the first time in history that Satan has been able to confuse or deceive people. Even in New Testament times, there are instances where foolish men were easily deceived by someone who could perform magic tricks. There is no reason to believe that—at least initially—those left behind after the Rapture will even doubt that the Antichrist is sent from God. God, after all, is a generic term in common usage. Even the Bible refers to Satanic deities like Baal or Molech as "gods" with a small "g."

IS THE UN THE GOVERNMENT OF THE ANTICHRIST?

In many respects, it seems to qualify. But the UN is not the revived Roman empire spoken of by the prophet Daniel. It serves as an intriguing prototype, but it isn't the final form of world government. The UN, for all its treaties and legalese, is a paper tiger. There is plenty of talk about giving it a standing army, a military budget, manpower and equipment. But it isn't the empire the Bible predicted, and it never will be.

---

[55] Revelation 13:4 NASB.

The United Nations is only the first step. Once the mechanisms are all in place, the UN will join its predecessor, the League of Nations, on the scrap heap of history. The UN represents an idea—one much loved by globalists, but doomed to failure.

TOO MANY CHIEFS, TOO FEW BRAVES

The crisis in Bosnia highlighted the flaws in the UN organizational table. Same principles apply to Somalia, Rwanda, Iraq or any of the other trouble spots the UN has tried to bully into submission. The problem is, there are too many diplomats, not enough decision makers. It is too political, too fragile, too unwieldy to function as a dictatorship as profound and universal as the one predicted by Scripture. But it does point the way.

POLITICS ABHORS A VACUUM

Despite its weaknesses, the UN has accumulated vast power. Its collapse is inevitable, and the power vacuum left by its demise will be filled. Even as the UN struggles with international defiance of its conventions and decrees, another global government is waiting and watching for its opportunity.

When the time comes, it is likely its leader will point to the necessity of maintaining existing treaties. But, he will argue, true global leadership will require a political post strong enough to usher in the brave "new world order" the UN founders worked so diligently to create. His plan will compensate for the deficiencies built into the UN system. He will have all the answers, and the world will gladly rally 'round his flag.

A wise man once said, "You can turn a cucumber into a pickle, but you can never turn a pickle back into a cucumber." The need for global government is established in the minds of enough people to make global government inevitable. The world's political system has already made the transformation. The popular sentiment is, "We're already in a pickle, and we need somebody to clean up this mess before we annihilate ourselves."

The Bible identifies the government of the Antichrist as a revived form of the Old Roman Empire. The only government with the economic, political and military power to step into the power vacuum left by the collapse of the UN is currently in the final stages of transformation.

BUILDING HIS POWER BASE

Following the Rapture, it's reasonable to assume there will be considerable confusion among men. After all, millions have disappeared, and nobody knows where. Instead of seeing this mass disappearance as the culmination of The Great Hope of Christianity, the world will see it as the Great Fear. Will I be next? It isn't difficult to imagine the whole world casting a fearful glance skyward, wondering if some cosmic beam will take them to who knows where.

But the Antichrist will have the answer to where everybody else went. Not the true answer, but one that is plausible enough and will calm the fears of

those left behind. Maybe, having pulled off his resurrection act, he'll claim that he was somehow
involved. Or, maybe he'll just explain it away. But
the Bible is clear on one point. He'll be believed and
eventually hailed as God. Having satisfied the fears
of a global population, he will be catapulted into a
position of global prominence. The leaders of nations
will have no choice but to submit to his will. After all,
they're only people, too. The last disappearance was
no respecter of rank. To their mind, everyone was
vulnerable to a repeat of the Great Vanishing—
including them. The Bible says that the Antichrist
will select as his power base ten nations that were for-
merly part of the Roman Empire. The prophet Daniel
makes that point clear.

Ten nations of Western Europe! There is some passage of time between the revelation of Antichrist and
the beginning of the Tribulation Period. Taking over
the world—even under these extraordinary circumstances—takes time. There's an old axiom that goes,
"Rome wasn't built in a day." It was true in ancient
times. It will also apply to the Revived Roman Empire
under Antichrist. But, thanks to modern mass communication, it won't take a generation, either.

CHAPTER 9

MORE BEASTS THAN A ZOO

Revelation Chapter 13 introduces

us to the beast, then another beast,

and throughout there is a theme of

yet another beast. Confused yet?

Don't be.

The Apostle John is continuing a theme first begun by the Prophet Daniel in the Old Testament. Remember, John is obeying the Lord's command to write down what he saw. Imagine for a second that you are a man who lived in the 1st century AD. Now imagine seeing a wide-screen Technicolor movie of the Gulf War, for example. Remember, you are working from a 1st century perspective. Now, using that perspective, describe what you are seeing. You've never seen a machine. In your world, everything that moves without being pulled by a horse, rolled down a hill, or shot from a bow is alive. Neither Daniel nor John was given the interpretation of the things that they saw, just the vision. In each case, the interpretation was sealed up until the generation to whom it was addressed had come into being.

> "As for me, I heard but could not understand; so I said, 'My lord, what will be the outcome of these events?' And he said, 'Go your way, Daniel, for these words are concealed and sealed up until the end time. Many will be purged, purified and refined; but the wicked will act wickedly, and none of the wicked will understand, but those who have insight will understand.' "[56]

So when the time came for them to describe the things they saw, concepts like machines, helicopters, tanks, and so on, were described in 1st century terms. Helicopters became "locusts," tank battles became "many horsemen," nuclear exchanges became "fire and brimstone," and so on. We'll discuss this further

---

[56] Daniel 12:8–10.

when we explore these specifics, but keep in mind that a "beast" in John's world was anything that defied conventional description.

OH, AND THE OTHER KIND OF BEAST...

Both Daniel and John also saw political systems and leaders that they described using the term "beast." In this case, however, "beast" (θηρίον), *therion,* is used to describe something bestial. The Greek word means "a wild animal," but it is also a metaphor for a wild, savage, ferocious man. The Lord uses "beast" metaphorically to convey how He views the system as well. The government of Antichrist is all of that—wild, savage, ferocious, bestial—and so that is how it is portrayed. But it isn't as complicated as it sounds.

THE BEAST FROM THE SEA

> "And I saw a beast coming up out of the sea, having ten horns and seven heads, and on his horns were ten diadems, and on his heads were blasphemous names" (Revelation 13:1).

John sees this beast coming up "out of the sea." This beast is a gentile leader of a gentile system. John didn't call it a beast because it was a Gentile. It comes up out of the sea of nations. In Daniel Chapter 7, the prophet records a dream that he had in which he saw the rise and fall of four gentile world empires. Each was char-acterized as a beast coming from the sea of nations.

> "In the first year of Belshazzar king of Babylon Daniel saw a dream and visions in his mind as he lay on his bed; then he wrote the dream down

and related the following summary of it. Daniel said, 'I was looking in my vision by night, and behold, the four winds of heaven were stirring up the great sea. And four great beasts were coming up from the sea, different from one another. The first was like a lion and had the wings of an eagle. I kept looking until its wings were plucked, and it was lifted up from the ground and made to stand on two feet like a man; a human mind also was given to it. And behold, another beast, a second one, resembling a bear. And it was raised up on one side, and three ribs were in its mouth between its teeth; and thus they said to it, "Arise, devour much meat!" After this I kept looking, and behold, another one, like a leopard, which had on its back four wings of a bird; the beast also had four heads, and dominion was given to it. After this I kept looking in the night visions, and behold, a fourth beast, dreadful and terrifying and extremely strong; and it had large iron teeth. It devoured and crushed, and trampled down the remainder with its feet; and it was different from all the beasts that were before it, and it had ten horns.' "[57]

So, the beast from the sea is the political part of the Antichrist's system. Satan is a counterfeiter. So he has an "unholy trinity" that consists of himself, the Antichrist (the political–religious beast) and the false prophet (the religious–political beast). Don't get alarmed, we'll take a look at him in a few minutes.

---

[57] Daniel 7:1–7 NASB.

Our beast in Revelation 13:1, then, is the Antichrist.

BY THE NUMBERS

He has ten horns, seven heads, and ten crowns. The ten horns represent the ten European nations that form his political power base. Daniel also was given the vision of the Antichrist, and he specifically asked the revealing angel to interpret its meaning. The angel told him:

> **"As for the ten horns, out of this kingdom ten kings will arise; and another will arise after them, and he will be different from the previous ones and will subdue three kings."**[58]

The Apostle John's vision had seven heads. Again, this is in harmony with Daniel's interpretation in which the Antichrist subdues three kings. Ten nations, seven heads. Still with me? The ten diadems of John's vision are ten crowns. Although three of the "**kings**," or national leaders, are "subdued" in some way by Antichrist, the national identities of all ten nations remain. It isn't a case in which three nations get the boot from the Antichrist's power base. All ten nations remain, but three of the leaders, who possibly disagree with his agenda, find themselves out of a job.

During World War II, Hitler annexed Austria. He ran it, controlled it, and all the orders came directly from Berlin, but Austria, as a political entity, remained. Austrians didn't become Germans; they just took their orders from Germany. By way of explanation, Hitler subdued the leader of Austria, but Austria itself remained.

---

[58] Daniel 7:24 NASB.

BEAST FROM THE EARTH

Revelation 13:11 introduces us to the second member of Satan's unholy trinity, the false prophet. John makes it clear that this is not the same fellow we met in verse 1, but that he is still a beast.

> **"And I saw another beast coming up out of the earth; and he had two horns like a lamb, and he spoke as a dragon."**

Just as the sea of nations are gentile, the use of the "earth" (land) is representative of Israel. "Land" with the definite article and not otherwise defined always refers to Israel. Israel is the Promised Land. It is the place where God chose to put His earthly Throne. It is the place where the Messiah will rule during the Millennial Kingdom.

So, the false prophet is not a Gentile.

The earth [land], which will one day be the inheritance of God's chosen people, is used symbolically to identify the false prophet as a Jew.

Notice that the false prophet has horns as well—he has two horns like a lamb, but speaks like a dragon. Jesus Christ is the Lamb of God, the sacrifice that takes away the sins of the world. The dragon is Satan. That gives us the religious perspective of the false prophet. He will be a Jew, who is a counterfeit messiah, but his doctrine comes straight from Satan.

THE THIRD MEMBER OF THE UNHOLY TRINITY

The third member, of course, is Satan himself. The revealing of the Antichrist which is described in

2 Thessalonians Chapter 2 tells us that he comes "in accord with the activity of Satan." It is Satan that energizes the Antichrist. It is Satan that gives the false prophet his doctrine. Satan is the one who enables both members of the unholy trinity to "speak great things," perform "lying miracles, signs and wonders" and call down fire from heaven, *etc.* So now we've identified all the lead players in the final chapter of mankind's greatest drama.

THE FIRST SEAL

The Tribulation Period is divided into a series of 21 Judgments, all of which take place in chronological order. Each of the Judgments is subdivided into one of seven types: the Seal Judgments, the Trumpet Judgments, and the Bowl Judgments. Each succeeding Judgment upon the earth is more terrible than the one before. It is a gradual process that starts somewhat slowly and increases in frequency and intensity until, finally, as Jesus promised in Matthew 24:22, if He didn't return to put an end to them, not a single human being would survive.

> **"And I saw when the Lamb broke one of the seven seals, and I heard one of the four living creatures saying as with a voice of thunder, 'Come.' And I looked, and behold, a white horse, and he who sat on it had a bow; and a crown was given to him; and he went out conquering, and to conquer."[59]**

[59] Revelation 6:1, 2 NASB.

This First Seal begins the seven-year ride of the Antichrist. The white horse in the ancient world was symbolic of conquest. The bow symbolizes his control over the weapons of war. The crown identifies him as the one who will eventually be accepted as king of the world. And, with the breaking of the First Seal, he begins his conquest of all kindreds, tongues and nations.

PEACE, PEACE, WHEN THERE IS NO PEACE

For most of the 1990s a kind of false peace has existed in the Middle East between Israel and her closest enemy, the Palestinians. The PLO negotiated an agreement to end 46 years of violence on September 13, 1993. The statement of principles called for a small autonomous area for the Palestinians in the West Bank town of Jericho and the Gaza Strip. The agreement called for limited self rule, confined to the areas of education, law enforcement and municipal government. The agreement ended the , but what is taking its place is far more ominous. Yasser Arafat's speech at the White House in September 1995 acknowledged the gains made by the PLO by calling for a Palestinian state with Jerusalem as its capital. Everyone politely applauded.

BACKED THE WRONG HORSE

Arafat and the Palestinians didn't make peace with Israel because they had suddenly had a change of heart. The Oslo Agreement actually saw its genesis in the betrayal by Arafat during the Gulf War of his principal benefactors and closest friends. The PLO received 98% of its annual operating budget from the oil–rich kingdoms of Saudi Arabia and Kuwait. Both countries hosted hundreds of thousands of Palestinian expatriates. Both countries extravagantly funded Arafat and his organization.

But then Saddam Hussein launched his brutal invasion of tiny Kuwait. His forces raped, pillaged, burned and murdered in a fashion reminiscent of the days of the Vikings. The CIA had developed intelligence that said his next target was the neighboring kingdom of Saudi Arabia. The United Nations authorized a multinational military force to push Iraq back inside its own borders.

Saddam began launching Scud missiles against Israel, hoping to prompt an Israeli response that would bring other Arab countries into the war on Iraq's side.

So great was Arafat's hatred of Israel that he turned his back on his principal benefactors and Arab "brethren" and publicly embraced the Iraqi leader and his aims. He issued statements of support for Iraq and totally ignored the victims of Iraq's aggression—simply because Saddam planned to attack Israel.

After Iraq's defeat, the infuriated Saudis and Kuwaitis withdrew all financial support for the PLO. They evicted hundreds of thousands of Palestinians from their borders, creating an immense refugee problem. Much of the money those Palestinians had earned in those countries had been sent home to help family members in Jordan and Israel. It all dried up, even as the population of refugee camps in Jordan swelled to overflowing. Arafat was broke, and he was in trouble. It was time for a new strategy.

ARAFAT—THE NOBEL PEACEMAKER

Overnight, Yasser Arafat transformed himself. One day, he was the world's chief terrorist, the backstabber who betrayed his closest friends, and the man most dedicated to the destruction of Israel. The next, he was a statesman, a peacemaker, and the man most likely to bring peace to the troubled Middle East. Few things concentrate the mind of a terrorist so wonderfully as being cut off from all funding. He began negotiating with his sworn enemy, Israel. Not because he had a change of heart, but because he needed a change of bankers. Of course the world immediately forgot his betrayal and the obvious reasons for his peace overtures. He shared the Nobel Peace Prize, was received as a head of state around the world, and became the most important man on earth, to listen to his apologists.

AN "INFERIOR PEACE"

Arafat has made it clear that regardless of what the outcome of the final status talks with Israel would be, he would declare the creation of the Palestinian independent state by May 1999. In 1997, Arafat signed the Hebron Protocol. In it he pledged his government to "Preventing incitement and hostile propaganda, as specified in Article XXII of the Interim Agreement."

Fifteen months later, Arafat gave an interview to Egyptian Orbit TV. In the interview Arafat repeated his support for the 1974 ten–point phased plan for Israel's destruction. He told the Egyptian television audience, "When the prophet Muhammad made the Khudaibiya agreement, he agreed to remove his title 'messenger of Allah' from the agreement. Then, Omar bin Khatib and the others referred to this agreement as the 'inferior peace agreement.' Of course, I do not compare myself to the prophet, but I do say that we must learn from his steps and those of Salah a–Din. The peace agreement which we signed is an 'inferior peace.' The conditions [behind it] are the Intefada, which lasted for seven years.' "

THE KOREISH TREATY

Arafat was referring to an agreement made by Muhammad with the Arabian tribe of Koreish. That deal was supposed to last for ten years. Muhammad broke it after only two years. He used that time to consolidate his forces and grow stronger than his enemy. *Salah a–Din* [Saladin] is the Muslim leader who, after a cease–fire, declared a jihad against the Crusaders and captured Jerusalem. During the same interview, Arafat also told Egyptian television, "We respect agreements the way that the prophet Muhammad and Salah a–Din respected the agreements which they signed."[60] In other words, the peace deal is a delaying action until Arafat can betray his word again.

---

[60] Egyptian Orbit TV, April 1998.

ENTER THE ANTICHRIST

The First Seal coincides with the signing of a seven–year peace treaty between Israel and her enemies, according to Daniel 9:27.

> "And he will make a firm covenant with the many for one week, but in the middle of the week he will put a stop to sacrifice and grain offering; and on the wing of abominations will come one who makes desolate...."[61]

A "**week**," as we've already seen, is a *shabua*, or a sabbatical week of seven years. Daniel tells us that the signer of that covenant is the Antichrist. He is the "**prince of the people**" that destroyed Jerusalem and the Temple (Daniel 9:26). The city and Temple were destroyed in AD 70 by the Roman legions under Titus, who eventually became the leader of the Roman Empire. The Antichrist is the leader of the Revived Roman Empire. From the moment that the ink is dry on that false peace deal, Planet Earth's final chapter begins. The Bible tells us that exactly 2,520 days later, Jesus Christ will return to earth to put an end to the madness before the remaining vestiges of humanity are extinguished.

A RELATIVE LULL IN THE ACTION

There is a period of relative quiet for the next three and one–half years while the Antichrist concentrates his efforts on consolidating his power. During that time Israel lives in a period of relative quiet.

---

[61] Daniel 9:27a NASB.

Somehow work begins on the reconstruction of the Third Temple on the Temple Mount. The false prophet gets moving on converting the whole earth to his new apostate "Christian" religion. Satan works behind the scenes, deceiving and conniving until the whole earth accepts his counterfeit unholy trinity as being legitimate. And in heaven, the Church enjoys the Marriage Supper of the Lamb.

STAGE FIVE

CHAPTER 10

THE CHARGE OF THE RED HORSE—

THE WAR OF ARMAGEDDON BEGINS

"And another, a red horse, went out;

and to him who sat on it, it was granted to

take peace from the earth, and that men

should slay one another, and a great sword

was given to him" (Revelation 6:4).

THE END OF PAX ANTICHRISTO

The purpose of the Second Seal is to shatter the Pax Antichristo. The rider on the red horse starts a series of battles that, when taken together, represent the War of Armageddon.

The Second Seal unleashes the unthinkable—an all-out war that will escalate to global nuclear war. The rider on the red horse is given this horrifying assignment and the tools necessary to implement his appointed destiny. First, notice that it was given to him to take peace from the earth. This is a point that is almost universally overlooked by the interpreters of the Apocalypse. In order for him to take peace away from the earth, it follows that the world was at peace until this point in the seven-year Tribulation history.

This is such an important moment in future history, with such enormous consequences, that many major prophecies converge upon it. I will take up some of those prophecies now.

JOHN'S EYEWITNESS ACCOUNT

As I shared in my last book, *The Apocalypse Code,* John the Apostle was commanded to write about only the things he saw, heard and felt.[62] All the things we will examine in the Book of the Revelation are the written accounts of a 1st century eyewitness who struggled to describe the marvels of 21st century technology.

---

[62] Hal Lindsey, *The Apocalypse Code* (Beverly Hills, CA: Western Front Publishing Company, Ltd.), 1997.

The Apostle describes the opening of the Second Seal and the Divine command to the Red Horse to charge forth and take peace from the earth. Its rider is not just to take peace from the earth, but his purpose is to cause "mankind to slaughter one another...." The Greek word is σφαξοῦσιν from the verb σφάζω. It means "to butcher, slaughter or massacre someone." This is also a purpose clause which reveals that peace is taken from the earth for the very purpose that mankind should butcher each other. And in the remainder of the Revelation's Seal, Trumpet and Golden Bowl Judgments—mankind does this to himself with ruthless skill.

He is given a great sword with which to slaughter himself. The context is not difficult to understand. The sword is a symbol of weapons of war. It was in John's day, and it is now. But notice a "great" (μέγας) sword is given to him. The meaning of the Greek word, together with John's prophetic code words, means weapons of enormous destructive power, or as we call them today, weapons of mass destruction. In the providence of God, these weapons now exist at just the right time in history for this to be fulfilled. What a "coincidence"!

It is a sad fact of history that mankind's greatest creativity has been spent on developing weapons with which to destroy himself with greater efficiency.

THE MAN OF "PEACE"

Many Bible expositors argue that the Tribulation is marked from the beginning by wars of conquest started by the Antichrist. The Bible doesn't support that view. The rider on the white horse, whose career was launched by the breaking of the First Seal, carries a bow—but he isn't brandishing arrows. He apparently conquers by supernatural diplomacy backed by the threat of power. During the first three and one–half years of the Tribulation, political intrigue and the manipulation of the global economy largely accomplish the conquests of the Antichrist.

THE GREAT COUNTERFEIT— DANIEL'S ACCOUNT

The reason for the world's adoration of the Antichrist is that he brings peace to the earth during the first three and a–half years of Daniel's "70th Week." He comes on a white horse, which is a symbol of a Conqueror. But Daniel foretold long ago the Antichrist's method of conquest. In the original Hebrew text, Daniel predicted **"and by means of peace, he will destroy many...."**[63] Because of his success as a peacemaker, John predicts how the world will respond: **"Men worshiped the dragon** [Satan] **because he had given authority to the beast, and they also worshiped the beast** [Antichrist] **and asked, "Who is like the beast? Who can make war against him?"**[64]

PEACE AND SAFETY— EZEKIEL AND PAUL'S ACCOUNT

For most the of first three and one–half years, the nation of Israel will have rested from the constant state of war

---

[63] Daniel 8:23, literal translation from the Hebrew Masoretic text.

[64] Revelation 13:4 NIV.

that was its normal experience from its rebirth in 1948.
That fact is made clear by the reference found in Ezekiel
Chapter 38. In verse 10, God refers to Israel at the
time the Battle of Gog and Magog begins as **"a land
of unwalled villages."** This clearly would indicate a
time of peace, even without the rest of the verse,
which says that Israel, at the midpoint in the
Tribulation is "at rest," living securely without walls,
bars or gates.

Antichrist will have guaranteed Israel's peace and
safety with the signing of the fateful covenant predicted by Daniel.[65] Abraham's children, descended
from both Ishmael and Isaac, will apparently be at
peace with each other for the first time in 4,000
years. But the Apostle Paul forewarned that this, in
and of itself, would be the sign that all hell is about
to break loose, **"While people are saying, 'Peace
and safety,' destruction will come on them suddenly, as labor pains on a pregnant woman, and
they will not escape."**[66]

SO WHO IS GOG?

The red horseman rides immediately to Moscow, and
sets in motion the first in a great series of global campaigns orchestrated by Satan himself. His goal is to
destroy the last earthly reminder of the God of the
Bible—Israel. The Church is already gone. The Holy
Spirit's restraint of lawlessness in the world is also
gone. All that remains to remind him that he has not

[65] Daniel 9:27.

[66] 1 Thessalonians 5:3 NIV.

yet eradicated all remaining traces of the truth about God from Planet Earth is God's special creation, the nation of Israel.

Ezekiel reveals how God will allow Satan to use the tools already in place—Islam's hatred of the descendants of Isaac and Russia's need for a secure power base in the Middle East. But, God's purpose is to reveal Himself to a remnant of His children and bring them to faith in Him. Ezekiel predicts that this will be accomplished when the Messiah delivers them from the invading hordes led by Gog, of the land of Magog, the prince of Rosh, Meschech and Tubal.

It is easy to establish who this power is. The first clue Ezekiel repeats three times. He will come from the extreme or uttermost north of Israel.[67] There is only one nation to the extreme north of Israel—*Russia.*

Second, he will be a descendent of the ancient tribes of Magog, Meshech, Tubal and a later people named after the combination of these people—*Rosh* or *Rus.* *Rosh* is a Hebrew term, which is translated as an adjective in the King James Version, but is in fact a proper noun. These peoples became known as the Scythians, who are the modern ethnic Russians.

The third clue is the time the Russian people will rise to power. Ezekiel clearly identifies the time: **"After many days you will be called to arms. In the latter years you will invade a land that has recovered from war, whose people were gathered from many nations to the mountains of Israel, which had long**

---

[67] Ezekiel 38:6, 15; and 39:2.

been desolate. They [Israel] **had been brought out from the nations, and now all of them live in safety.**"[68] In other words, this refers to our present era, which began with the rebirth of the nation of Israel.

GOG'S INVASION FORCE

Ezekiel gives a role call of those who will fight alongside of the Russians in this invasion of Israel: "**Persia, Cush and Put will be with them, all with shields and helmets, also Gomer with all its troops, and Beth Togarmah from the far north with all its troops—the many nations with you.**"[69]

Persia is modern Iran. It is perfectly accurate that Persia/Iran is named as the leading ally of Russia. Since the Islamic Fundamentalists of the Shiite sect took over Iran in 1979, there have been three overriding goals guiding the Ayatollahs of Iran: first, to become the spiritual leader of the Muslim world; second, to destroy the nation of Israel and recapture Jerusalem; and third, to drive the West out of the Middle East.

Iran is rapidly becoming the most dangerous nation in the world, next to Russia. With Russian help they are very near going operational with intercontinental ballistic missiles tipped with thermonuclear, chemical and biological warheads.

Cush is a son of Ham who is one of the three sons of Noah. Cush is the father of the Black African people.

---

[68] Ezekiel 38:8 NIV.

[69] Ezekiel 38:5, 6 NIV.

In fact, his name in Hebrew means black. Today, many Black African nations have embraced Islam. They will be part of this confederacy called by Daniel the King of the South.

Put is also a son of Ham. He is the father of the North African people who dwell mostly along the southern shore of the Mediterranean Sea. Today they are the peoples of Libya, Algeria, Tunisia, Morocco and Mauritania. All of these nations are predominantly Muslim. They will be part of Russia's great invasion force.

The tribes of **Gomer** started out in the region of modern Turkey. They later spread to the Balkans and Europe. This most likely refers to the Muslim dominated population of Turkey.

"Beth Togarmah from the far north with all its troops" refers to a tough people who spread to the north of the Caucasus Mountains and eastward across the vast region that is now Armenia, Azerbaijan, Uzbekistan, Turkmenistan, Tadzhikistan, Kazakhstan, *et al.* These are heavily populated with Muslims and are former Republics of the Soviet Union. These Muslims look today to Iran for spiritual and economic leadership. They will be part of the great invading force, armed and led by the Russians like all the rest.

THE HOOK IN THE JAW?

Ezekiel uses an allegorical picture to predict that God will mislead Russia into a catastrophic strategic miscalculation. The symbol of the hook refers to a kind of bridle used in that day. It had metal hooks that would dig into a mule or jackass's jaw if the animal got stubborn and wouldn't follow its master. A few jerks on the lead and the beast would become obedient. So God says He is going to lead Russia forcibly into this disastrous invasion.

Since the collapse of the Soviet Union, the Russian government has continued to collapse into chaos. Russian business is largely run by Russian organized crime. At the present, those who have the money dictate politics. It's the present world system's golden rule: "He who has the gold makes the rules." The Russian mob is just as interested in conquering the Middle East to obtain a cheap source of oil as any preceding legitimate government of Russia ever was. And what remains of the Russian political system has a vested interest in hanging on to what little authority it still has.

WOUNDED PRIDE CAN BE LETHAL

A number of old politicians and military officers cannot bear Russia's present humiliation. They passionately want to restore Russia as a super power. Economically, Russia is a disaster. But from the standpoint of the invention and creation of military weapons, the Russians are world class. And the legacy of the Soviet Union years is the most formidable arsenal of weapons in history. More than once Russian leaders have reminded Western leaders of this point when they felt ignored in world decisions.

Russia has, in keeping with the above purpose, opted to go to the Third World, where it can exercise great authority and lead it. Now the dominant power bloc in the third world is the oil–rich Muslim nations. So it fits into Russian overall strategy to help the Muslims in order to establish leadership over them, and to form a power base from which they can build toward super–power status.

Russia now has an huge financial stake in Iran. Iran supplies hard currency in exchange for weapons, particularly weapons of mass destruction, which Russia has in abundance. But Iran won't do business with the Russian mob, so Russian–organized crime is as dependent on the political system as the system is on the mob's control of business. And Iran is the key for both, if they want to survive and prosper at this time.

WHEN ALLAH HOOKED GOG

But the real reason for Russia's "hook in the jaw" is the pact signed with Iran in February 1991. In the aftermath of the chaotic disintegration of the Soviet Union, Russia greatly feared that the southern Republics of the former union, which are heavily populated by Muslims, would catch the Islamic Fundamentalist Revival "fever." Even the Muslims of the little state of Chechnya caused great disruption when they had an Islamic–motivated revolt.

Russia rightly foresaw the threat of this happening in a Muslim–dominated Republic like Kazakhstan, which had a large percentage of the former Soviet Union's nuclear–tipped ICBM's buried in silos on its soil. Iran's fanatical dedication to Islam was and is very attractive to Muslims who had been forced into an atheistic society for some 70–plus years.

The Russian leaders knew that in order to get what they wanted Iran would have to get what it wants. So, Moscow offered Tehran a deal it couldn't refuse. In February 1991, a pact was made between Russia and Iran.

Some of the salient points of this pact are these: (1) Russia agreed to supply Iran with both materials and world–class nuclear and missile experts. They would help Iran build its own nuclear warheads and delivery systems. (2) In exchange, Iran agreed not to encourage in any way an Islamic revival in the former Soviet Republics and also not to interfere with Russia's efforts to put down any such revivals. (3) Russia agreed to fight alongside Iran against the West in the event they invaded Iran, invaded other Muslim nations of the region, or sought to interfere with the internal affairs of the Muslim nations of the region.

THE HOOK WAS SET

This pact virtually ensured that Russia would one day be drawn into war against the West on behalf of its Muslim allies. The liberation of Jerusalem and Palestine, in their minds, is an internal affair of the Muslim world. To the devout Muslim, the annihilation of Israel is a just and necessary act to restore the honor of Allah's armies and to resanctify Jerusalem as the third holiest site in Islam.

Ezekiel foresaw Russia's role of having an enormous arsenal and supplying the Muslim Confederacy for war, then leading them into war: "**Get ready; be** prepared, you and all the hordes gathered about you, and take command of them."[70]

A DEVELOPMENT TO LOOK FOR

There is every probability that the next president of Russia will be a military strongman who will be bent upon reestablishing Russia's former super–power status. He will appeal to the people's patriotism and love for Mother Russia in order to get their votes. He will promise to rid Russia of the Russian Mafia. He will raise up the demoralized military and rebuild it into a proud, combat–ready armed force. This will fit into the predicted role for the Russians. The cryptic name of the coming Russian strongman is *Gog*. He is probably a general whose name you have heard on CNN. I believe that this military strongman must come before the events of Ezekiel take place.

TARGET—ISRAEL

It is predicted that the Islamic republics will finally have their revenge against Israel for daring to claim possession of the Third holiest site in Islam— Jerusalem. Almost against its better judgment, Russia will find herself at the head of a vast northern army running headlong toward their date with destiny on the mountains of Israel. Ezekiel foresaw the situation: **"And you will come from your place out of the remote parts of the north, you and many peoples with you, all of them riding on horses, a great assembly and a mighty army; and you will come**

---

[70] Ezekiel 38:7 NIV.

up against My people Israel like a cloud to cover the land. It will come about in the last days that I shall bring you against My land, in order that the nations may know Me when I shall be sanctified through you before their eyes, O Gog...."[71]

JESUS WARNED OF WHEN WAR WOULD BREAK OUT

Jesus Christ also spoke of this critical point of future history: "So when you see standing in the holy place 'the abomination that causes desolation,' spoken of through the prophet Daniel—let the reader understand—then let those who are in Judea flee to the mountains. Let no one on the roof of his house go down to take anything out of the house. Let no one in the field go back to get his cloak. How dreadful it will be in those days for pregnant women and nursing mothers! Pray that your flight will not take place in winter or on the Sabbath. For then there will be great distress, unequaled from the beginning of the world until now—and never to be equaled again. If those days had not been cut short, no one would survive, but for the sake of the elect those days will be shortened."[72]

A SINISTER SYLLOGISM

So, since the Second Seal of Revelation Judgments has to occur when world peace is broken, and since

---

[71] Ezekiel 38:15, 16 NIV.

[72] Matthew 24:15–22 NIV.

Ezekiel describes Russia and the Muslim Confederacy invading Israel at a time of peace, and since Jesus predicts that the event which triggers the beginning of the invasion is the abomination that causes desolation at the midpoint of the Tribulation, the Second Seal must occur at the middle of the Tribulation.

The Apostle Paul revealed what blasphemous act is the abomination that causes desolation: **"He will oppose and will exalt himself over everything that is called God or is worshiped, so that he sets himself up in God's temple, proclaiming himself to be God."**[73]

When the Antichrist of Rome takes his seat in the Holy of Holies of the Jews' rebuilt Temple and then declares himself to be God, all hell is going to break loose. This is the **"abomination that causes desolation"** predicted by Daniel the Prophet and referred to by Jesus the Messiah.[74]

This will be the sign that immediately precedes the Russian–led Islamic invasion of Israel.

DANIEL'S PREVIEW OF THE WAR'S BATTLE PLAN

> **"At the time of the end the King of the South** [the Muslim Confederacy] **will engage him** [the False Prophet of Israel] **in battle, and the King of the North** [Russia] **will storm out against him with chariots and cavalry and a great fleet of ships. He** [the Russian Commander] **will invade many**

---

[73] 2 Thessalonians 2:4 NIV.

[74] Matthew 24:15; Daniel 9:27 and 12:11.

countries and sweep through them like a flood. He will also invade the Beautiful Land [Israel]. Many countries will fall, but Edom, Moab and the leaders of Ammon [Jordan] will be delivered from his hand. He will extend his power over many countries; Egypt will not escape. He will gain control of the treasures of gold and silver and all the riches of Egypt, with the Libyans [Put] and Nubians [Cush] in submission. But reports from the east and the north will alarm him, and he will set out in a great rage to destroy and annihilate [the] many [Israelis]. He will pitch his royal tents between the seas at the beautiful holy mountain. Yet he will come to his end, and no one will help him."[75]

Ezekiel details how the King of the North, will be destroyed:

"You will advance against my people Israel like a cloud that covers the land. In days to come, O Gog, I will bring you against my land, so that the nations may know me when I show myself holy through you before their eyes.

"This is what the Sovereign LORD says: Are you not the one I spoke of in former days by my servants the prophets of Israel? At that time they prophesied for years that I would bring you against them.

"This is what will happen in that day: When Gog attacks the land of Israel, my hot anger will be aroused, declares the Sovereign LORD. In my zeal and fiery wrath I declare that at that time there shall be a great earthquake [violent shaking] in the land of Israel. The fish of the sea, the birds of the air, the beasts of the field, every creature that moves along the ground, and all the people on the face of the earth will tremble at my presence. The mountains will be over-turned, the cliffs will crumble and every wall will fall to the ground.

"I will summon a sword against Gog on all my mountains, declares the Sovereign LORD. Every man's sword will be against his brother. I will execute judgment upon him with plague and bloodshed; I will pour down torrents of rain, hailstones and burning sulfur on him and on his troops and on the many nations with him. And so I will show my greatness and my holi-ness, and I will make myself known in the sight of many nations. Then they will know that I am the LORD.

"Son of man, prophesy against Gog and say: 'This is what the Sovereign LORD says: I am against you, O Gog, chief prince of Meshech and Tubal. I will turn you around and drag you along. I will bring you from the far north and send you against the mountains of Israel. Then I will strike your bow from your left hand and make your arrows drop from your right hand. On the mountains of Israel you will fall, you and all your troops and the nations with you. I will give you as food to all kinds of carrion birds

and to the wild animals. You will fall in the open field, for I have spoken, declares the Sovereign LORD.' "[76]

The Prophet Joel also speaks of this awesome catastrophe: " **'I will drive the northern army far from you, pushing it into a parched and barren land, with its front columns going into the eastern sea and those in the rear into the western sea. And its stench will go up; its smell will rise.' Surely he has done great things."**[77]

In the next chapter, we will look at how this war impacts the rest of the world. This information is revealed in the opening of the Third, Fourth, Fifth and Sixth Seals. Thank God right now that you won't be here if you have received the gift of pardon that Jesus died in your place to purchase for you, for the real horror is about to begin.

---

[76] Ezekiel 38:16—39:5 NIV.

[77] Joel 2:20 NIV.

CHAPTER 11

THE DISINTEGRATION OF THE NEW WORLD ORDER

SORROWS GO EXPONENTIAL

The breaking of the Second Seal, Jesus warns,

is the "beginning of sorrow," as rendered in the

King James Version. The New American Standard

renders it this way: "For nation will arise against

nation, and kingdom against kingdom; there will

be earthquakes in various places; there will also be

famines. These things are merely the beginning

of birth pangs."[78]

---

[78] Matthew 24:8 NASB.

As we've already seen, Jesus used a consistent system of prophetic symbols, so that the generation to whom He was speaking would be able to break the prophetic code. Birth pangs are a universal experience. Every parent who ever lived knows that birth pangs get closer together and more intense as the birth approaches. That's why new parents to this day time the contractions so that they know when it is time to load up the car and head to the hospital.

Labor usually begins somewhat slowly. First there are a few pains, nothing regular, but certainly recognizable. These pains are almost random at first. There may be a few, and then nothing for hours, or even days. Then there are a few more series of pains. Finally, they develop a pattern. Fifteen minutes apart, then twelve, then ten, and so on. As the birth becomes imminent and the intervals of pain get down to two or three minutes, each pain becomes more intense. Just before birth, the pains close to only a few seconds apart.

Once the Second Seal is broken, however, Planet Earth's contractions follow the same natural pattern. After all, the One who used this symbol is the same One who created the birthing system to begin with.

THE CHARGE OF THE BLACK HORSE— ECONOMIC COLLAPSE AND FAMINE

The Third Seal unleashes war's most common companion—famine. But this is famine on a scale never seen in recorded human history.

"And when He broke the Third Seal, I heard the third living creature saying, 'Come.' And I looked, and behold, a black horse; and he who sat on it had a pair of scales in his hand. And I heard as it were a voice in the center of the four living creatures saying, 'A quart of wheat for a denarius, and three quarts of barley for a denarius; and do not harm the oil and the wine.' "[79]

Throughout the history of warfare, famine has been a constant companion of war. In both world wars in this century, there was widespread rationing. Following World War I, Germany's economy was so decimated that it took a wheelbarrow full of German marks to buy a loaf of bread. Currency was so devalued, it was more valuable as stove kindling than it was as money. The value of the mark dropped from roughly four to the dollar to a ratio of billions to the dollar. So devalued was it, in fact, that by 1919 comparisons were worthless because the mark devalued faster than the exchange rate could be published. A wealthy German who had a million marks on deposit in 1914 against his retirement found that, only five years later, his nest egg would barely buy a slice of bread.

And who could forget the pitiful images of women and children picking through the rubble of bombed-out German cities in 1945, hoping to find a potato or an undamaged can of food? War always brings on famine...for the loser.

---

[79] Revelation 6:6.

Of course, although there was rationing, the victorious Allies didn't suffer anything like the deprivation of the Germans, Japanese or Italians. Even at the lowest point of the Allied effort, there was enough to eat. One might have needed a ration card to buy butter; there were "Meatless Tuesdays," and the like; but nobody—not the British, not even the French—suffered widespread famine on a scale reminiscent of the defeated Axis powers.

But the rider on the black horse presents a different kind of famine. It is global in scope and divided into two characteristics. John sees two specific groups:

First, **"a quart of wheat for a denarius, and three quarts of barley for a denarius."** The reference to a "quart of wheat" or "three quarts of barley" points roughly to the minimum intake of food to sustain life for a single day—that is to say, a day's food for a "denarius." A "denarius" is the Biblical equivalent to a day's wages. So, putting it together, we see that a day's wages will be just enough for a day's food for one person. Not one family, but one person.

And second, **"do not harm the oil and the wine."** Oil and wine are symbols of wealth. These are luxury items. The sorts of things you would find in the pantry of a wealthy family. To the average family in John's day, oil and wine were reserved for special events. Few people could afford them as part of their weekly grocery budget.

So we see that the rider on the black horse takes prosperity from the earth and replaces it with famine. This kind of rationing is defined in the Book of Ezekiel. God instructed Ezekiel to go on a starvation diet. It doesn't sound very appetizing:

> **"And your food which you eat shall be twenty shekels a day by weight; you shall eat it from time to time. And the water you drink will be the sixth part of a hin by measure; you shall drink it from time to time. And you shall eat it as a barley cake, having baked it in their sight over human dung."**[80]

The average family on a global basis will barely have enough to eat, but the supremely wealthy will still live well. Especially the arms dealers—at least for a time.

God begins this Judgment by separating the wheat from the chaff. At least some of those afflicted early will cry out to God in desperation.

> **"I will go away and return to My place. Until they acknowledge their guilt and seek My face; in their affliction they will earnestly seek Me."**[81]

Eventually, however, even the wealthiest will see their time of judgment. By the time the rider on the black horse has finished his ride, the plight of post World War I Germany will look like comparative prosperity!

> **"Come now, you rich, weep and howl for your miseries which are coming upon you. Your riches have rotted and your garments have become moth-eaten. Your gold and your silver have rusted; and their rust will be a witness against you and will consume your flesh like**

[80] Ezekiel 10:12.

[81] Hosea 5:15.

fire. It is in the last days that you have stored up your treasure! Behold, the pay of the laborers who mowed your fields, and which has been withheld by you, cries out against you; and the outcry of those who did the harvesting has reached the ears of the Lord of Sabaoth."[82]

THE CHARGE OF THE PALE HORSE WITH THE DEATH ANGEL

As I've already pointed out, the Book of the Revelation is written in chronological order. Each of the events is sequential. Once the Black Horseman has taken prosperity from the earth, then war's other constant companion raises its ugly head.

"And when He broke the Fourth Seal, I heard the voice of the fourth living creature saying, 'Come.' And I looked, and behold, an ashen horse; and he who sat on it had the name Death; and Hades was following with him. And authority was given to them over a fourth of the earth, to kill with sword and with famine and with pestilence and by the wild beasts of the earth."[83]

The "ashen" horse is translated from the Greek word χλωρός (chloros), which actually is more of a sickly green, yellowish, pale color. The color of the very sick, and the color of the newly dead. This horseman has the horrific mission of unleashing hell itself on earth.

---

[82] James 5:1–4.

[83] Revelation: 7:7.

A TIME LIKE NO OTHER

This horseman has the authority to kill a fourth of mankind. His ride extends all the way through the Tribulation but it begins with the breaking of the Fourth Seal. During his tenure, he is given specific tools with which to work:

- The sword, or, military weapons

- Famine, or starvation. A day's work, as we've already seen, only buys a day's food for one. Not everybody will be able to work. What about the sick, the old, mothers and small children? This is a famine so terrible that Jesus said that unless it was miraculously shortened by His return, eventually everyone on earth would succumb. Think of the madness and atrocity such a famine will bring. Especially in a world without the restraining influence of God's Holy Spirit in the world. Without the Holy Spirit, it will truly be an "every man for himself" scenario.

- Pestilence. The dictionary defines "pestilence" as epidemic, incurable disease. We are already experiencing a foretaste of that which is to come. The following comes from a recent report from my television program, *The International Intelligence Briefing*:

    "A new killer viral infection has investigators baffled. At least 30 babies have died from an intestinal virus that is sweeping the island nation of Taiwan. The virus has already infected more than 2,000 babies on the island. The United States has sent a team of investigators from the US Center for Disease

Control to try and help isolate the virus before it spreads. The government of Taiwan has authorized a special epidemic task force to work full time on this latest killer. Officials have ordered nursery schools and kindergartens closed in an effort to stop the spread of the infection. The virus is called EnteroVirus 71. It is believed to be a strain of influenza, and this is the deadliest outbreak seen to date. Complications from the virus include encephalitis, meningitis, and acute inflammation of the heart muscle. It is spread by contact with other victims. We live in a world that used to boast that infectious disease is a thing of the past. Now, newer and newer strains threaten to be the killers of the future. Diseases like hantavirus, Lyme Disease, Hong Kong's bird flu, AIDS, flesh eating disease and Hepatitis C are all products of this generation. Complications from these diseases are creating mutant strains of other killers that defy conventional antibiotics."[84]

THE BEASTS OF THE EARTH

Although the world has always known plagues, there is something unique about the pestilence described here. It also makes reference to the "beasts of the earth." There are two ways of looking at this passage—both of them literal. One is the obvious—wild beasts are wild beasts, after all. The word ζῷον (*zoon*) literally means "a living being" or, "an animal, brute or beast." We are already witnesses to an unusual phe-

---

[84] *International Intelligence Briefing,* June 11, 1998.

nomenon in which mountain lions are killing tourists in California, elephants are "zoning out" for no apparent reason at zoos or in cities like Bombay, wolves are attacking people in cities all over the world, *etc., etc.* And, there is no doubt this verse refers to that phenomenon squared. Animals long domesticated are also turning on their owners or just anybody who might get in the way. But the Greek word is just as accurate in context when read as "living being" or even "living organism."

THE CELL FROM HELL

Pfeisteria, the mysterious "red tide" that has nearly bankrupted fishing industries along the East Coast is also a living being. This tiny organism kills by producing a poison a thousand times more toxic than cyanide. As the deadly red tide approaches the shore, eyewitnesses report seeing fish leap out of the water in an effort to escape what is literally being boiled alive. As a fish killer, Pfeisteria is already scary enough. But in the lab, it has also shown a taste for human blood. Fishermen and lab technicians who've come in contact with it have suffered symptoms like memory loss, crippling muscle weakness and extreme weight loss. Pfeisteria, or a mutated version of it, is also suggested in other Divine Judgments described in the Book of the Revelation, and elsewhere.

> "And the second angel poured out his bowl into the sea, and it became blood like that of a dead man; and every living thing in the sea died."[85]

---

[85] Revelation 16:3.

Pestilence was used to convince the spiritually blind in the past. In one particularly spectacular instance, Aaron made a pronouncement upon Egypt during the Exodus.[86]

Remember, John was describing what he saw using 1st century terms. God may again literally turn the water into blood during the Tribulation, but John says it became "like the blood of a dead man" and that mysterious pestilence killed every living thing in the sea. It certainly fits the profile of Pfeisteria to a "T."

DON'T LOOK AWAY

The ride of the four horsemen gives us an overview of the whole of the Tribulation Period. They lay out, in general terms, how it will all unfold. In just these few verses, we see a picture develop that is so horrifying, it's tempting to look away in terror. That must have been John's reaction, as each of the visions of the horseman is preceded by the angelic command, "Come." The KJV renders it "Come and see." The Textus Receptus includes the primary word, βλέπω ("see, or behold") that carries with it a sense of being present and observing experientially. One way of defining this word βλέπω is, "to discover by use, to know by experience." What an experience it must have been!

---

[86] "Then the Lord said to Moses, 'Say to Aaron, "Take your staff and stretch out your hand over the waters of Egypt, over their rivers, over their streams, and over their pools, and over all their reservoirs of water, that they may become blood; and there shall be blood throughout all the land of Egypt, both in vessels of wood and in vessels of stone" ' " (Exodus 7:19).

THE FIFTH SEAL—MARTYRDOM

Revelation Chapter 13 tells us that during the reign of Antichrist, Satan will have a special authority not usually granted him, and never granted him during the Dispensation of the Church Age. He will be given power to take the lives of the saints of God at will. Now, there have always been persecutions of the Church, and certainly many millions have been martyred. But this time, it's different. For all the millions that were martyred in the past, many millions more lived in peace. Not so during the Tribulation period.

> "And it was given to him to make war with the saints and to overcome them; and authority over every tribe and people and tongue and nation was given to him."[87]

There are but two Seals left in this overview of a world under the authority of Antichrist. The Fifth Seal is the war against those who accept Christ during this hellish period.

> "And when He broke the Fifth Seal, I saw underneath the altar the souls of those who had been slain because of the word of God, and because of the testimony which they had maintained; and they cried out with a loud voice, saying, 'How long, O Lord, holy and true, wilt Thou refrain from judging and avenging our blood on those who dwell on the earth?' And there was given to

[87] Revelation 13:7.

**each of them a white robe; and they were told
that they should rest for a little while longer,
until the number of their fellow servants and
their brethren who were to be killed even as they
had been, should be completed also."**[88]

A great number of those who accept Christ during
the Tribulation will be killed. That is the price paid
for eternal life by those who fail to accept the free gift
offered them on this side of Hell on earth. The gift
given the Church is incomprehensibly generous
when contrasted against the price paid by those
saints who reject the Mark of the Beast. (We'll discuss
this in greater detail later). In the Church Age, all
that is necessary to avoid the scenes we have already
discussed is a simple faith in Christ. Once the Age of
Grace draws to a close, those sinners who come to
Christ will receive their full wages for their previous
rejection of this most precious gift.

**"For the wages of sin is death, but the free gift
of God is eternal life in Christ Jesus our Lord."**[89]

Before we go on, perhaps you might want to take a
look at your own spiritual condition. It's not too late.
At least, not yet. There is still time to escape all that
is coming on the earth. But not much. The Rapture
could come, and this present Age of Grace could vanish before you finish reading the words on this page.
Consider your options carefully.

---

[88] Revelation 6:9.

[89] Romans 6:23.

THE SIXTH SEAL—TERROR

The opening of the Sixth Seal is even worse, if you can imagine it, than the one before. Like birth pangs. A madness of abject, indescribable horror falls upon the whole earth. Nobody is exempt. The horrors of the Tribulation find their way into the hearts and minds of everyone, from the greatest to the least.

> **"And I looked when He broke the Sixth Seal, and there was a great earthquake; and the sun became black as sackcloth made of hair, and the whole moon became like blood; and the stars of the sky fell to the earth, as a fig tree casts its unripe figs when shaken by a great wind. And the sky was split apart like a scroll when it is rolled up; and every mountain and island were moved out of their places. And the kings of the earth and the great men and the commanders and the rich and the strong and every slave and free man, hid themselves in the caves and among the rocks of the mountains; and they said to the mountains and to the rocks, 'Fall on us and hide us from the presence of Him who sits on the throne, and from the wrath of the Lamb; for the great day of their wrath has come; and who is able to stand?' "**[90]

Up until this point, Russia and its Muslim allies have been the aggressors and have run rampant through the Middle East and Africa virtually unopposed. They have wreaked havoc with the Antichrist's world order.

---

[90] Revelation 6:8.

Now they face the fury of a mobilized Western army. It is at this point, I believe, that the Antichrist will launch his nuclear counterattack. He covers his counterattack by launching the greatest salvo of nuclear–tipped ICBM's imaginable. This will surely be answered by Russian and Muslim ICBM's, which will have been programmed to launch on warning. "Launch on warning" means that the missiles are launched automatically when an attack is detected by radar or satellite.

Until this future point in history, we only know by computer model and theory the horrible consequences of multiple thermonuclear detonations in close proximity of time and space. I believe John gives us an eyewitness account of what will happen.

"And the sky was split apart like a scroll when it is rolled up" is a perfect 1st century description of the atmospheric effect from a nuclear blast. The atmosphere is pushed back on itself from the tremendous overpressure of the blast. Catastrophic damage is done both as the atmosphere is compressed on itself and pushed away and then when it returns with almost equal force into the vacuum.

John saw **"stars falling from heaven like ripe figs."** The word rendered "stars" could be translated "asteroids" or "meteors" with equal accuracy, depending on the context. As I noted in my book, *Apocalypse Code,* as well as elsewhere in this book, John was a 1st century man trying to describe a 21st century war.[91] This simply can't be emphasized strongly enough. It proves

[91] Hal Lindsey, *The Apocalypse Code* (Beverly Hills, CA: Western Front Publishing Company, Ltd.), 1997.

the inspiration of the Holy Spirit. John just didn't possess the technical vocabulary necessary to describe clearly the events he witnessed. But for the generation to whom the Revelation would be relevant, it reads like tomorrow's headlines.

These verses certainly stand in contrast to the heady days of Satanic joy described in Revelation 13:4. Nobody is saying **"Who is like the beast, and who is able to wage war with him?"** anymore.

If you haven't settled your business with God, you could change your eternal destiny from hell [both this "hell on earth" and the eternal place of torment] to eternity in heaven right now. Just bow your head and tell God that you know you fall short of His standards. Then receive the gift of pardon that Jesus purchased for you with His Blood. And I'll see you at the Rapture.

CHAPTER 12

THE DESTRUCTION OF EARTH'S ECOLOGY

"The earth will be completely laid waste

and completely despoiled, for the LORD has

spoken this word.... The earth is also POLLUTED

by its inhabitants, for they transgressed laws, violated

statutes, broke the everlasting covenant. Therefore,

a curse devours the earth, and those who live in it

are held guilty. Therefore, the inhabitants of the

earth are burned, and few men are left"

(Isaiah 24:3, 5, and 6).

THE SEVENTH SEAL UNVEILS SEVEN GREATER TERRORS

The scene shifts to heaven for the opening of the Seventh Seal. There is a solemn atmosphere with an ominous silence in heaven for about 30 minutes. Mankind, still reeling from the devastating blows of the first six Judgments, is given opportunity to reflect and repent.

The opening of the Seventh Seal actually unleashes the next series of seven Judgments, which are entrusted to seven archangels of highest rank. John testifies to what he saw: "And I saw the seven angels who stand before God; and seven trumpets were given to them." When these Trumpets sound, the catastrophes will go beyond anything ever imagined by mankind. This series of Judgments exponentially increase the level of devastation on earth.

PRAYERS MORE POWERFUL THAN ALL WEAPONS

The Seventh Seal opens up the mightiest power of all. John writes:

> "Another angel, who had a golden censer, came and stood at the altar. He was given much incense to offer, with the prayers of all the saints, on the golden altar before the throne. The smoke of the incense, together with the prayers of the saints, went up before God from the angel's hand."[92]

---

[92] Revelation 8:3, 4 NIV.

This mighty archangel stands before the heavenly golden altar of incense, which is before the Throne of the Almighty God. The altar constructed by Moses for Israel's Tabernacle was copied from this one.

The prayers of all the believers are mingled with heavenly incense and offered up to God. These prayers contain the martyrs' and the suffering saints' cries for relief and justice. The answer to these prayers is the Seven Trumpets and Seven Golden Vials. These release such total destruction that unless the Lord Jesus Christ returned to rescue His own, the planet would no longer be able to sustain life.

God wants the world to know that there is a certain judgment coming upon all those who commit injustices and atrocities against His children. At this future point He acts in response to all their prayers and cries. The world, still reeling from the blows of the opening of the six Seals, is about to be hit with the most devastating blows of all history, never to be equaled again.

John describes the most fearful event yet: "**And the angel took the censer; and he filled it with the fire of the altar and threw it to the earth; and there followed peals of thunder and sounds and flashes of lightning and an earthquake.**"[93]

The prayers of God's children move the Throne of God to act, and woe to those rejecters of GOD who come under the flood of fire they release from the altar.

---

[93] Revelation 8:5 NASB.

John, under the inspiration of the Holy Spirit, uses some grippingly effective visuals, wouldn't you agree? Most of us have seen stock footage of the mushroom cloud rising over either Hiroshima or the South Sea test islands. But John, who lacked exposure to the science of the 20th century, didn't have the background to describe such things. Even so, he did an inspired job with the understanding and words available to a 1st century man.

THE TRUMPETS—THE EFFECTS OF GLOBAL NUCLEAR WAR!

When the first angel blows his Trumpet, it may sound like a trumpet to John, but it will reverberate on Planet Earth in the form of a thousand Hiroshimas. Fully a third of the world's vegetation will be burned up and all the grains will be destroyed. Have you seen the old footage from the nuclear tests in the '50s? Usually they are played back on documentaries or news stories when they want to provide a visual image of a nuclear detonation. You remember, the trees are knocked sideways, a house dematerializes, and the shock wave rolls out from the epicenter. Terrifying. That footage was made back in the '50s to convince Americans of the need to build bomb shelters, back during the hottest days of the Cold War. It was so effective that more than 100,000 bomb shelters were actually constructed in back yards all across America. So far, nobody has needed one. And with today's weapons, it's unlikely they would do much good anyway.

John's vision is just as graphic as that old bomb footage; it's simply on a much grander scale.

THE MYSTERY OF AN UNNATURAL MIXTURE

"And the first sounded, and there came hail and fire, mixed with blood, and they were thrown to the earth; and a third of the earth was burned up, and a third of the trees were burned up, and all the green grass was burned up" (Revelation 8:7).

In a nuclear detonation, humidity in the air is instantly compressed into water and driven straight up into the freezing temperatures of the upper stratosphere. It then is instantly frozen and falls back to earth as giant chunks of ice. John saw **hail and fire, mixed with blood.** Nothing in John's experience, not even a volcanic eruption, would create ice and at the same time create fire. And the fact that **blood** is mingled with the **fire** and **ice** is self–explanatory. John saw them **thrown** to earth, which is exactly what happens following a nuclear blast. They don't just fall. The shock wave literally throws the ice, debris, bits of burning material and so forth in all directions, as it falls back toward earth. Picture the scene. See it in your mind. Now describe it. How much different is what you described from John's description. And remember, you have the technical vocabulary to describe these things; he didn't. I'd say he did a masterful job.

WANT RESPECT? GO NUCLEAR!

John saw **a third of the earth, grass and trees burned up.** Consider how many nations are currently nuclear. Recently Pakistan and India joined the nuclear club. North Korea is planning to join as well. Pyongyang just reneged on a deal not to manufacture fissionable material because North Korea noticed that these former Third World countries are getting the respect that used to be shown only to Russia, China, France, Great Britain and the United States.

The kind of destruction John describes is what today's "think tanks" theorize will happen if all of these nations let a few of their nukes fly at their favorite enemies. Not enough to blow the world to smithereens, but certainly plenty to burn a third of the world's vegetation, and so on. Remember, the earth's surface is five–sixths water and only one–sixth land mass.

The results are horrific, almost unimaginable. A third of all remaining trees are burned up. This means that the air will become super polluted and the trees that cleanse and add oxygen to our atmosphere will be gone when needed most. At the time of this writing, a large part of Southeast Asia is blanketed by the choking smoke and soot caused by out–of–control fires in the rain forest area of Indonesia. The same condition is also occurring in the southern part of the United States and all of Mexico because of out–of–control fires in the rain forest of southern Mexico. Just think of the catastrophe when a third of the whole planet's trees are on fire.

An even greater tragedy is that **all of the green grains are burned up**. With famine raging in many parts of the world and scarcity of food everywhere else, this will seal the doom of millions. Perhaps the lucky ones will be those who die in the explosions.

Thus begins the *first* of the Trumpet Judgments. It's already not a pretty picture, but the worst is yet to come.

REVIVING FORGOTTEN FEARS

The latest nuclear race in South Asia is putting everyone on alert that the Cold War might be over, but the threat remains. In an article called "Nuclear Tests Bring Up End of World Fears," *USA Today* profiled the attitude of Americans who did not grow up under the shadow of nuclear annihilation, like those of us who remember the '50s and '60s.

"Most veterans of America's great Cold War bomb scare had put it behind them, and beaten their fallout shelters into so many ploughshares—a wine cellar, a Smithsonian exhibit and a "mom" shelter. But now, with atomic bombs again being test–fired by two antagonistic nations, these people face some of the fears that resulted in the shelters.

Once more, Americans like Paul Meints, Vera Howey and Sheryllee Lowe are thinking about an explosion too bright to look at, followed by a mushroom cloud; about a hometown's place on a list of bombing targets; about being too poor to afford a home fallout shelter. India and Pakistan, the newest and poorest nuclear powers, have brought to life a concern as old as the bomb itself—annihilation. Some Americans shrug off the crisis as an incomprehensible dispute on the other side of the world that involves no important US ally or interest. But for others—especially those over 40—the standoff on the Indian subcontinent evokes a time when a majority of US adults told pollsters they thought they'd die in a nuclear war with the Soviet Union. It didn't matter where you were: in Eureka, Kansas, identified by a Boston economist as the nation's safest place; or in Washington, DC, you were certain of obliteration 100 times over in case of war. It was a spooky time. Great missiles with nuclear warheads sat in concrete silos 17 stories below the Great Plains. Bombers were aloft every hour of every day, waiting for the order to fly toward Moscow. On the ground, airmen slept next to runways in bunkers called "mole holes," ready to sprint to their aircraft. Even the ground crews wore side arms."[94]

But the Book of Revelation was written 2,000 years ago—before nuclear weapons had even been dreamed of—and John had no such illusion of eventual "peace and safety" from the unlocked power of the atom. He knew *exactly* what he saw—and there was no doubt in his mind that God was able to accomplish it.

A BIGGER CLUB THAN WE THINK

An NBC report profiled those nations who either are nuclear or have significant nuclear programs. Among those unofficial nuclear powers NBC identified are Libya, Iran, Iraq, Syria, Egypt, Belarus, North Korea and Israel. In addition to those are the two newest official powers, India and Pakistan.

[94] *USA Today*, June 6, 1998.

Every single one of those nations can be found in Ezekiel Chapter 38's account of the Battle of Gog–Magog. NBC's reporters really did not have to do as much research as they did. All they really needed to do was look into a 2,500–year–old manuscript to obtain today's breaking news!

The most interesting accounts were those of Iran and Iraq. Together, they make up the old Persian Empire identified in Ezekiel 38:5. NBC says of Iran:

> "Iran's pursuit of nuclear weapons predates the Islamic revolution of 1979, though efforts by the Shah's regime are not thought to have come to much. However, with a highly educated core of engineers to draw on, the ayatollahs recommitted themselves to the pursuit of the nuclear prize and, according to US intelligence estimates, may be as close as three years from grasping it. Though Iran denies it is trying to build a bomb, senior Iranians privately have cited the large, unacknowledged Israeli nuclear arsenal and efforts in neighboring Iraq—another bitter foe—as a rationale for their own program. Persistent rumors of Iranian agents scouring the former Soviet Union for nuclear material have failed to be confirmed. However, the fear of just such a security lapse led the United States and Russia to conclude a pact to secure the former Soviet arsenal. Iran's main outside source of nuclear weapons material is thought to be China, though recent allegations have centered on alleged Russian efforts to conceal nuclear weapons cooperation behind civilian nuclear technology

deals. Moscow denies such cooperation, but refuses to back out of lucrative deals to help build Iranian nuclear power stations."[95]

The report also details Saddam Hussein's efforts to obtain the Bomb:

> "The extent and sophistication of Iraq's nuclear weapons program came as something of a shock to the West when the Gulf war's guns fell silent. Such fears existed before the war as well, though during the long Iran–Iraq war the United States and other Western powers were loath to do anything that would benefit Teheran. Israel, however, was convinced enough of Iraq's potential as a nuclear threat that it dispatched jets to destroy an Iraqi research reactor at Osirak in 1981. After the Gulf war, United Nations weapons inspectors, who won access to Iraqi facilities as part of the war's armistice, found a program and found that Baghdad's scientists had been on the verge of success. Iraq's program was aided enormously by former Soviet and Chinese technology. Since the war, however, UN inspectors constantly have been frustrated in their efforts to verify the destruction of Iraq's nuclear infrastructure."[96]

What makes this story truly interesting is the list of countries contained in the report that are all working together in this vast nuclear conspiracy. The Bible makes no mention of the United States as a partici-

---

[95] MSNBC *Special Report*, May 28, 1998.

[96] ibid.

pant in the end–time conflict. It doesn't mention the United Kingdom, or France or Argentina, or Canada. All these countries are great nations with significant wealth, prestige and power. Instead, the Bible refers to the same nations—by name—as the NBC report. The great nations that do get Biblical reference are the Kings of the East, (China, India, Pakistan—all openly nuclear), Russia (Gog–Magog), Libya, Egypt, Iran, Iraq and so on. All of them have remained obscure, impotent little Third World nations for most of recorded modern history. Now, at the appointed time, they are front–page news. Right on schedule!

SEALED UNTIL THE APPOINTED TIME

Although John records the blowing of the first Trumpet 2,000 years ago, the mechanism necessary for bringing his catastrophic vision to life wasn't even invented until 1945! Even then, 1,900 years after he recorded the effects of a nuclear holocaust, it wasn't yet possible. Now it's the most likely scenario, according to NBC. That's why even the great Reformers like Calvin and Luther saw Revelation as a mysterious book of symbols and confusing images, while even the most casual observer today can see right past the imagery and into the substance.

Both Daniel and John were instructed to seal up much of what they saw, reserving the interpretation for the generation to whom it would be obvious: "I was about to write; and I heard a voice from heaven saying, 'Seal up the things which the seven peals of thunder have spoken, and do not write them.' "[97]

> "But as for you, Daniel, conceal these words and seal up the book until the end of time; many will go back and forth, and knowledge will increase."[98]

It should be apparent to even the most casual of readers that *this* is the generation in which knowledge has increased to the level necessary to understand the differences between symbols and substance. This is the generation in which many will experience John's eyewitness testimony—to their everlasting regret!

---

[97] Revelation 10:4b.

[98] Daniel 12:4.

CHAPTER 13

MEANWHILE, BACK ON EARTH...

While all this is going on in heaven,

on earth Satan is doing his best to maintain

control of the planet he has finally gotten

complete control of. As far as he is concerned,

he has at last realized his ambition first

articulated in Isaiah Chapter 14.

> "But you said in your heart, 'I will ascend to heaven; I will raise my throne above the stars of God, And I will sit on the mount of assembly In the recesses of the north. 'I will ascend above the heights of the clouds; I will make myself like the Most High.' "[99]

Satan has wanted to be worshiped as god on earth, but the God of heaven has thwarted him at every turn through those believers who rejected Satan's authority and recognized him for who he was, due to the revealing influence of the Holy Spirit. But in this future time, Satan thinks victory is within his grasp. The Church is gone. Most of Israel is in unbelief and it's time for him to accept the worship that is due him. The whole rest of the world thinks he is "the man," but God's chosen people are the principal target. If he can get them to worship him, he wins!

DO YOU MIND IF I SIT DOWN?

The Bible says that the Antichrist, Satan's proxy, will march into the rebuilt Temple at Jerusalem, walk into the Holy of Holies, take his seat at the Mercy Seat on the Ark of the Covenant, and proclaim himself to be God. The Jews apparently tolerate him as a sort of god to the Gentiles. The Apostle Paul calls him the **"son of destruction," "who opposes and exalts himself above every so–called god or object of worship, so that he takes his seat in the temple of God, displaying himself as being God."**[100] Although

---

[99] Isaiah 14:3–14.

[100] 2 Thessalonians 2:4.

Satan gained dominion over the earth when it was legally transferred to him by Adam at the Fall of Man, dominion isn't worship. And worship is what jars Satan's preserves! That's what he craves. He even tried to get Jesus, whom he knew was the Creator, to worship him while the Lord was in human form. He knew Jesus had come to redeem the earth from his dominion, and he tried to cut a deal.

> **"Again, the devil took Him to a very high mountain, and showed Him all the kingdoms of the world, and their glory; and he said to Him, 'All these things will I give You, if You fall down and worship me.' "**[101]

Of course, that didn't work. But Satan, for all the credit we give him, really isn't the sharpest tool in the shed! He continues to believe he has a chance to win, even though he knows as well as we do that the Bible writes him off in the last chapter.

So when he sits himself down on the mercy seat and demands to be worshiped as the Supreme God of Abraham, Isaac and Jacob, I suspect he is stunned by Israel's overwhelming rejection of him. The Bible says that a third of Israel will become believers and will enter into the Millennium. But it is hard to imagine even the most secular Jew buying into the idea of the God of Moses popping in for a visit.

I have a friend in Jerusalem named Gershon Salomon. He is not a believer in Jesus the Messiah, but he is certainly a believer that we have entered the

---

[101] Matthew 4:8, 9.

Messianic era. He heads the Temple Mount Faithful movement. That is an organization dedicated to rebuilding the Temple that the Antichrist will eventually claim as his throne. Gershon may well build this temple. His longing for the Messiah of Israel may result in his acceptance, at least temporarily, of the false prophet, who does claim to be Israel's long–awaited Messiah.

But I cannot see him, or any other devout Jew, entertaining the claims of the Antichrist for a split second! The Jews of the Tribulation Period might tolerate a god of the Gentiles, but there is only *one* God of Israel. The Old Testament says God *appoints* political leaders, but He doesn't take on the job personally.

Rather than obtaining the worship of God's own chosen, he is instead denounced as an abomination. And then the gloves come off! This event marks the beginning of the Great Tribulation that Jesus spoke of.

> "Therefore when you see the ABOMINATION OF DESOLATION which was spoken of through Daniel the prophet, standing in the holy place (let the reader understand), then let those who are in Judea flee to the mountains; let him who is on the housetop not go down to get the things out that are in his house; and let him who is in the field not turn back to get his cloak. But woe to those who are with child and to those who nurse babes in those days! But pray that your flight may not be in the winter, or on a Sabbath; for then there will be a great tribulation, such as has not occurred since the beginning of the

world until now, nor ever shall. And unless those days had been cut short, no life would have been saved; but for the sake of the elect those days shall be cut short."[102]

HELL HATH NO FURY LIKE THE ANTICHRIST SCORNED

Forced to deal with the Russian/Muslim invasion, the Antichrist breaks his peace treaty with Israel, and begins a systematic persecution of the Jews unlike anything ever seen. Hitler was an amateur compared to the Antichrist. Both had the same idea, but Hitler also had to contend with a two front war; all the while, keeping his campaign of murder out of the public eye. The Antichrist suffers no such constraints. Up until this point in time, the economy is good, unemployment is down, hedonism is the order of the day and the government only interferes if you're not partying hard enough. Sin reigns supreme on the earth, and the people like it!

> "They worshiped the beast, saying, 'Who is like the beast, and who is able to wage war with him?' "[103]

CHAOS—THE OPENING ACT

While his secret police begin rounding up the Jews who haven't yet escaped to the mountains, the Antichrist is busy on the global front, making sure

---

[102] Matthew 24:15–22.

[103] Revelation 13:4b.

that this doesn't happen again anywhere else. Satan is the author of the phrase, "If you can't beat 'em, buy 'em," and he sets that stage of his plan in motion while he still has time. If he's learned anything from history, he's learned this equation: Healthy economy + Really Big Lie + Weak, but Plausible Excuse + Someone Else to Blame = Social Control. It worked for Hitler. It seems to be working even better in the global arena. John describes it this way:

> **"And he causes all, the small and the great, and the rich and the poor, and the free men and the slaves, to be given a mark on their right hand, or on their forehead, and he provides that no one should be able to buy or to sell, except the one who has the mark, either the name of the beast or the number of his name."**[104]

This is the "Mark of the Beast," one of the most often quoted and least understood end–time prophecies of the Bible.

HOW MUCH FREEDOM WOULD YOU TRADE FOR SECURITY?

That was a question put forth on CNN following the Oklahoma City Bombing in 1995. By and large, nobody seemed to catch an implication hidden in the question. The question wasn't *would we trade freedom for security?* but rather, *how much?* The Antichrist carries it to the next level, now that the plateau has already been reached. His question is,

---

[104] Revelation 13:16, 17.

*how much economic security would you trade for free-
dom?* And the answer is, *how much will it take?* The
Mark of the Beast was something never before possible in history. Without the advent of computers, it was
impossible for any one man, or even any one system
of government, to control the buying or selling by
individuals on a global basis. Thanks to the currently
developing cashless society—ATM cards, MARC cards,
Electronic Funds Transfer systems, Value Added
Cards, and the like—cash is really little more than an
anachronism. Take the good old USA, for example.
What would happen if your Social Security number
were somehow erased from the system? You couldn't
work. You couldn't buy a car or a home—even for
cash. In fact, if you walked into an auto dealership
or real estate office with that much cash, you'd walk
out accompanied by agents of the IRS, ATF, DEA, *etc.*
The whole alphabet would be after you!

SOCIAL DEATH AND THE MARK

You can't even have telephone service connected
without a Social Security number! A good friend of
mine is from Canada. Jack is a writer who works
from time to time on projects for a publishing company out here in Los Angeles. Jack owns a home in
Canada. He has a brand–new car. He has credit
cards, a bank account, identification, and so forth.
Jack even served in the US Marines during the
Vietnam War, along with 44,000 or so other largely
forgotten Canadian veterans who went south to fight
to protect their own freedom, passing thousands of
north–bound Americans (including one future

President) who evidently wanted their freedom without personal cost. But when Jack tried to have a phone turned on in a temporary office he set up here, he wasn't able to do it until his Social Security number was verified. He couldn't even open a temporary bank account using cash. And he couldn't cash a check to open the account until he produced his Social Security number! This is a US Marine Corps veteran, not an illegal alien!

I say all that to say the system is already in place and functioning. It seemed like a good idea, at the time. But, whether it is a good thing or a bad thing all depends on who is in charge of the system.

With that in mind, what if your Social Security number were electronically eliminated? To all intents and purposes, you'd become "socially dead." That's the situation, as it stands, right now! The only thing necessary to implement the Mark of the Beast system is a mark...and a beast. Everything else is already here, in place, and waiting for the right moment in time.

WILL THAT BE HAND, OR FOREHEAD?

The Bible says that everyone will have to accept a mark in the right hand or forehead. The word translated "mark" means, literally, "graven." It conveys the sense of being "branded." The custom of the Hebrews, when they took a slave for life, was to mark them by driving an awl through their ear (see Exodus 21:6). In John's day, slaves were branded by their owners in a similar fashion. Accepting the mark of the Beast means you are sold into slavery—to Satan.

Without the mark, a person will be unable to engage in routine commerce—a kind of reverse Star of David. Anyone who accepts this mark during the Tribulation has already made his choice, and that choice will permanently disqualify its wearer from heaven.

The prefix 666 is added to your personal number to validate it. But you can't get the prefix until you swear allegiance to the Antichrist as God.[105] It isn't merely economic, it is a worship system. Accepting the mark is tantamount to a rejection of Jesus. A permanent, irreversible rejection.

> **"If anyone worships the beast and his image, and receives a mark on his forehead or upon his hand, he also will drink of the wine of the wrath of God, which is mixed in full strength in the cup of His anger; and he will be tormented with fire and brimstone in the presence of the holy angels and in the presence of the Lamb."[106]**

REMEMBER MAGOG?

It's at about this time that the northern alliance led by Russia makes its move. As we discussed in Chapter 10, all the necessary elements are already in place. The political alliances foreseen by Ezekiel are well–developed, and all that is necessary is an opportune moment to invade. It could well be that when the Antichrist begins his temper tantrum following

---

[105] Revelation 13:15.

[106] Revelation 14:10.

his rejection by the Jews, the Moscow–Tehran Axis decide the time is right. Or, they could move simply because this is when God says they will, and they think that "evil thought" described by Ezekiel in 38:10. At any rate, the Battle of Gog–Magog begins with a Big Bang. The prophet Joel describes the scene as the great northern alliance approaches the mountains of Israel.

> "Before them the earth quakes, the heavens tremble, the sun and the moon grow dark, and the stars lose their brightness. And the Lord utters His voice before His army; surely His camp is very great, for strong is he who carries out His word. The day of the Lord is indeed great and very awesome, and who can endure it?"[107]

THE SECOND TRUMPET SOUNDS

> "And the second angel sounded, and something like a great mountain burning with fire was thrown into the sea; and a third of the sea became blood; and a third of the creatures, which were in the sea and had life, died; and a third of the ships were destroyed."[108]

The first four Trumpet Judgments are essentially the result of the chaos begun by the Gog Magog invasion and counterattack. The Russian–Islamic axis nations have launched their invasion against Israel, and into Africa. The Antichrist, military dictator of the Roman

---

[107] Joel 2:10, 11.

[108] Revelation 8:9–11.

Empire, launched his ICBM arsenal against the invaders at the opening of the Sixth Seal. Ezekiel says the Russians are already at the mountains of Israel, much too close for intercontinental ballistic missiles to be of any defensive use to the Israelis. The Antichrist isn't fighting to defend Israel, anyway. He has already broken the treaty that would guarantee Israel's borders against invasion. The Antichrist is protecting the world's (his) oil reserves in the Middle East and hoping to use the excuse to eliminate a rival in the process. The strike is very effective against the Russian rear and homeland. Russia, like a wounded dog snapping in all directions, launches retaliatory strikes against Europe, China and the United States. Picture the scene! It appears as if the whole world is on fire. Hundreds of millions are vaporized, all over the planet. Some never saw it coming until it was there. The Russian homeland is a radioactive pit. The great steppes of the Russian breadbasket are polluted by radiation, and those who survive the nuclear conflagration have only starvation to look forward to.

THE THIRD TRUMPET

"And the third angel sounded, and a great star fell from heaven, burning like a torch, and it fell on a third of the rivers and on the springs of waters; and the name of the star is called Wormwood; and a third of the waters became wormwood; and many men died from the waters, because they were made bitter."[109]

---

[109] Revelation 8:10, 11.

The actual composition of the star called Wormwood is not clear. From the preposition used in Greek, it is clear that it is of extraterrestrial origin.

Several years ago, Jupiter was bombarded by a shower of comets. The cosmic fireworks display showcased the awesome destructive power of a collision between interplanetary objects.

At sunrise on June 30, 1908, the area near the Tunguska River in Siberia was the site of a tremendous explosion that had the force of a modern H–bomb and took place at an altitude of several miles. Though the explosion flattened trees for miles in all directions, no crater was formed, and aside from some microscopic nodules extracted from the soil, no recognizable fragments of an extraterrestrial object remain. Space scientists generally believe that the explosion was caused by a small comet that disintegrated in midair. However, there are no recorded meteoric strikes large enough to produce catastrophic damage.

John says that the name of the star is called Wormwood. That is an interesting choice of words. We all remember the Chernobyl disaster in the heartland of the Ukraine, at the headwaters of a series of rivers. Chernobyl was the breadbasket for the majority of the old Soviet Union, compounding the seriousness of that accident. The rivers were bitterly polluted by the accident. Many died from radiation sickness.

A rough translation of *wormwood* into Ukrainian would be "Chernobyl." What the choice of words does is provide us with a tiny preview of how much water could be polluted by a single incident. Whatever Wormwood actually is, it is an awesome display of God's power and a chilling picture of the judgment that is coming on the earth.

THE DESTRUCTION OF GOG—MAGOG

At that point, the Israelis let go with their own "secret" weapon. The Israeli Defense Forces have highly developed battlefield nukes called "neutron bombs." They are nicknamed "dial a nuke" in deference to the precision with which they can be programmed just before being deployed. These weapons can be used with sight of friendly troops, without inflicting friendly casualties. And they only destroy living flesh. An enemy caught at ground zero would be instantly vaporized, even with the opposing side close enough to witness the carnage with field glasses. These weapons are so new, so secret, and so deadly that few people outside of military circles even know such weapons exist. But God knew, and He told Zechariah all about them when he was given details of another, upcoming battle for Jerusalem.

> "Now this will be the plague with which the Lord will strike all the peoples who have gone to war against Jerusalem; their flesh will rot while they stand on their feet, and their eyes will rot in their sockets, and their tongue will rot in their mouth."[110]

---

[110] Zechariah 14:12.

Think about this! Before they can fall, their flesh is consumed, leaving only the skeleton to fall to the ground! In spite of all of this, still the surviving invaders push forward. Where else can they go? Behind them is a nuclear wasteland, before them, the mountains concealing their traditional enemy. To the north is the Antichrist and his army. To the south, more devastation. It is at this point that God Himself steps in and administers the coup d'grace.

> "Thus says the Lord God, 'Are you the one of whom I spoke in former days through My servants the prophets of Israel, who prophesied in those days for many years that I would bring you against them? And it will come about on that day, when Gog comes against the land of Israel,' declares the Lord God, 'that My fury will mount up in My anger. And in My zeal and in My blazing wrath I declare that on that day there will surely be a great earthquake in the land of Israel.' "[111]

Just imagine the scene now! This ranting, wild–eyed mob that once fielded an army of millions, equipped with the most up–to–date weaponry man has ever developed, who only days before were totally confident of victory, is now just a tiny remnant. They are the sole survivors of an entire society whose warlike traditions trace backward through time to the earliest traditions of the Mongol hordes, and the fierce Scythian calvary. And just when it couldn't get any worse,...

---

[111] Ezekiel 17:19.

"And with pestilence and with blood I shall enter into judgment with him; and I shall rain on him, and on his troops, and on the many peoples who are with him, a torrential rain, with hailstones, fire, and brimstone. And I shall magnify Myself, sanctify Myself, and make Myself known in the sight of many nations; and they will know that I am the Lord."[112] And so the curtain rings down on the proud confederation of nations whose leader once boasted as he struck the UN podium with his shoe, "We will bury you."

---

[112] Ezekiel 38:22, 23.

CHAPTER 14

WHAT MANKIND'S TECHNOLOGICAL SKILLS PRODUCE

BATTLE PLAN FOR MANKIND'S ULTIMATE NIGHTMARE

So, let's make a quick assessment of the War to this point, using Daniel's preview of the war's progress.[113] When the Antichrist of Rome gathers his Western armies to counterattack Gog and his Muslim allies, he will certainly launch nuclear missile strikes to cover his movements and halt their advance. The Russian–led forces will already be in Egypt, with expeditionary forces racing across North Africa and southward down Africa's East Coast. So, the Antichrist will target all troop concentrations and critical supply lines.

[113] Daniel 11:40–45, as explained in chapter.

This will cause an instant missile response by Russia and all of its nuclear–capable Muslim allies. In this kind of a situation, all of their missiles will have been placed on the "launch on warning" status, which means that when their satellites pick up the first sign of Rome's missiles launch, they will instantly respond also. Such allies as Pakistan, Iran, Iraq, Libya and Egypt will launch missiles before they are hit. As a result, most of the major nations of the earth suffer ICMB hits and are virtually destroyed. Europe, China and the US are all digging out from the rubble; entire cities and their surrounding areas have been wiped from the face of the earth.

THE JUDGMENT OF THIRDS

Notice something here. Even though God allows a third of the things judged to be annihilated, He allows two thirds to survive. During the Trumpet Judgments, one third of every vital thing of our planet is destroyed: a third part of earth's trees, vegetation and all grains is burned up (Revelation 8:7); a third of all sea vessels is destroyed (Revelation 8:8); a third of all living things in the sea is killed (Revelation 8:9); a third of all fresh water is poisoned (Revelation 8:10); and a third of all light from space will be blotted out by a "nuclear winter."

A WORD TO THE WISE

Perhaps the most terrifying revelation is that mankind and his own inventions wreak most of this global holocaust. God endowed man with great inventive capability, but instead of using it for good, he uses it to destroy his planet and himself. Man's most basic problem has never been a lack of intelligence or education, but a nature that is fallen and morally corrupted. Unless man experiences a new birth, in which he receives a miraculous birth of a new spiritual nature through which God communicates with him, he is doomed to the destructive influence of his fallen nature.

THE NUMBERS ARE INCOMPREHENSIBLE

Let's focus, for a second, on the mind–boggling statistics of human death here. We aren't even halfway through the Judgments that have yet to be delivered. The population of Planet Earth is roughly five and one-half billion people now. By the year 2002, there will be six billion. For the sake of illustration, I will use that figure.

This means that approximately two billion people have perished in the Judgment of the Fourth Seal! How many people is that? Put it this way. If those people were killed, one at a time, one person per second, the process would take about 65 years. Hitler and his henchmen were only able to wipe out 12 million in the camps. And he was using the most advanced technology ever developed for mass murder. Fifty–eight million perished during all of World War II, on all fronts, in all countries, from all causes. This includes not just the soldiers, but also civilians who perished from bombings, disease, starvation and death camps, *etc.* Two billion is *2,000 million!*

World War I used to be called "the war to end all wars." But even with its 38 million dead, it was only a dress rehearsal for World War II with its 58 million! So, how can any experience of past history prepare mankind for the death of more than four billion souls in less than three and one–half years? There are no words!

IT'S DARK OUT

There is something especially frightening to man when an unnatural darkness occurs in nature. But, what is described as taking place with the sounding of the Fourth Trumpet goes into the realm of utter terror.

The survivors who crawl out from under their shattered cities will find it cold, dark, and terrifying. The air that isn't poisoned with radioactive fallout will be a lung–searing, thick, choking soup of minute particles of debris produced by the multiple thermonuclear explosions. That is what the scientists call the "nuclear winter" effect. The debris kicked up into the atmosphere will turn day into night. Remember the images of Kuwait, just after Iraq set fire to its oil fields? I remember when I first saw those images on the news. In particular, I recall the words of the news anchor. He called it an "apocalyptic scene of biblical proportions." It was neither. It was ugly, but it pales in comparison to the Fourth Trumpet Judgment. **"And the fourth angel sounded, and a third of the sun and a third of the moon and a third of the stars were smitten, so that a third of them might be darkened and the day might not shine for a**

third of it, and the night in the same way."[114]

It astonishes me that people can view the Book of the Revelation as an allegory or as a book of symbols that have no prophetic meaning. Once you understand, from the *Apocalypse Code,* that John was a 1st century eyewitness of the beginning of 21st century events, it becomes understandable immediately.[115] It means exactly what it says, and it describes exactly what will happen. The Old Testament prophets foresaw the same effect, following the judgment of God on "the day of the Lord." Read the following prophecies carefully. Realize that these prophets had visions that were more than virtual reality. They actually saw the weapons of war that would not exist until the 20th and 21st centuries AD. Yet they had to describe them with their understanding of things that existed more than five centuries before Christ.

"Listen, a noise on the mountains, like that of a great multitude! Listen, an uproar among the kingdoms, like nations massing together! The Lord Almighty is mustering an army for war. They come from FARAWAY LANDS, from the ends of the heavens—the Lord and the weapons of his wrath—to destroy the whole country. Wail, for the day of the Lord is near; it will come like destruction from the Almighty. Because of this, all hands will go limp, every man's heart will melt. Terror will seize them, pain and

---

[114] Revelation 8:12.

[115] See author's book, *The Apocalypse Code* (Western Front Publishing Co., Ltd., Beverly Hills, CA), 1997.

anguish will grip them; they will writhe like a woman in labor. They will look aghast at each other, their FACES AFLAME. See, the day of the Lord is coming—a cruel day, with wrath and fierce anger—to make the land desolate and destroy the sinners within it. The stars of heaven and their constellations WILL NOT SHOW THEIR LIGHT. The rising sun will be DARKENED and the moon will NOT GIVE ITS LIGHT. I will punish the world for its evil, the wicked for their sins. I will put an end to the arrogance of the haughty and will humble the pride of the ruthless. I will make [MORTAL] MAN scarcer than pure gold, more rare than the gold of Ophir. Therefore I will make the heavens tremble; and the earth will shake from its place at the wrath of the Lord Almighty, in the day of his burning anger."[116]

"Blow a trumpet in Zion, and sound an alarm on My holy mountain! Let all the inhabitants of the land tremble, for the day of the Lord is coming; surely it is near, a day of DARKNESS and GLOOM, a day of CLOUDS and THICK DARKNESS. As the dawn is spread over the mountains, so there is a great and mighty people; there has never been anything like it, nor will there be again after it. To the years of many generations. A FIRE consumes before them, and behind them a FLAME burns. The land is like the garden of Eden before them, but

---

[116] Isaiah 13:4–13 NIV.

a desolate wilderness behind them, and nothing at all escapes them. Their appearance is
like the appearance of horses; and like
war–horses, so they run with a noise as of char-
iots. They leap on the tops of the mountains,
like the crackling of a flame of fire consuming
the stubble, like a mighty people arranged for
battle. Before them the people are in anguish;
all faces turn pale. They run like mighty men;
they climb the wall like soldiers; and they each
march in line, nor do they deviate from their
paths. They do not crowd each other; they
march everyone in his path. When they burst
through the defenses, they do not break ranks.
They rush on the city, they run on the wall;
they climb into the houses, they enter through
the windows like a thief. Before them THE
EARTH QUAKES, the heavens tremble, the sun
and the moon GROW DARK, and the stars lose
their brightness."[117]

I believe there is ample evidence for nuclear weapons
in these prophecies, and they dovetail into those of
the Revelation.

UNDERSTANDING DOUBLE–REFERENCE PROPHECIES

How do we know that these are prophecies about the
events of the Tribulation? Isaiah begins as an Oracle
against Babylon. There are several reasons that put

---

[117] Joel 2:1–10 NIV.

this in the period just before the Messiah comes in judgment on the earth. First the scope of this prophecy increases to include catastrophe upon the whole world, not just the region around Israel. Such statements as **"I will make MORTAL MAN scarcer than pure gold, and mankind than the gold of Ophir"** and **"for the stars of heaven and their constellations will not flash forth their light; the sun will be dark when it rises, and the moon will not shed its light. Thus I will punish the WORLD for its evil..."** all go beyond the scope of the Babylonian invasion of Israel in the 6th and 7th centuries BC. GOD did not judge the world then, either.

Also the use of a prophetic time code, "the day of the LORD." When this is connected with prophecies that include the whole world, and astrological phenomena that involve the whole planet, it is referring to the time that leads to the Second Coming of the Messiah, Jesus of Nazareth. Joel's prophecy clearly refers to that period, even though part of it was fulfilled at the day of Pentecost with the pouring out of the Holy Spirit.

Those who remain alive following this second phase of the War of Armageddon will find the world much like their hearts—cold, dark, lonely and without hope. It is a period beyond human comprehension. Jesus said it was like nothing the world had ever seen or would ever see again. And what is about to come is far worse, folks.

WOE, WOE, AND WOE AGAIN!

> "And I looked, and I heard an eagle flying in midheaven, saying with a loud voice, 'Woe,

> woe, woe, to those who dwell on the earth,
> because of the remaining blasts of the trumpet
> of the three angels who are about to sound!' "
> (Revelation 8:13).

Before the next three Trumpets are sounded, a warning is sounded, as if what has already transpired is not bad enough. Still, men are unconvinced and continue to look to the Beast to save them. I can imagine the scene, terrible as it is. Not too unlike the images presented in the Hollywood movie *Mad Max*—a nightmare world of every man for himself. No shame, no thought for anything other than personal survival. And in the midst of it all, little groups of "religious" zealots, perhaps dancing around a fire and chanting to the very one who is responsible for their situation. Satan has no more control over what is happening on the earth at this point than he ever did. Satan merely had dominion over the minds of unsaved men, but God has always been in control of natural forces.

> "For our struggle is not against flesh and blood,
> but against the rulers, against the powers,
> against the world forces of this darkness,
> against the spiritual forces of wickedness in the
> heavenly places" (Ephesians 6:12).

THE FIFTH TRUMPET

> "And the fifth angel sounded, and I saw a star
> from heaven which had fallen to the earth; and
> the key of the bottomless pit was given to him"
> (Revelation 9:1).

The Fifth Trumpet sounds with the expulsion of Satan from heaven. The identification of Satan in this passage is not hard to make. Isaiah foresaw this development in exactly the same manner described by John.

> "How you have fallen from heaven, O star of the morning, son of the dawn! You have been cut down to the earth, you who have weakened the nations!"[118]

Many people mistakenly believe that throughout human history, Satan has already been banished from heaven, or that he reigns in some kind of kingdom in hell. That isn't true. Satan has always had access to the Throne of God, where he serves as the principle accuser of the saints of God.

> "Now there was a day when the sons of God came to present themselves before the Lord, and Satan also came among them."[119]

Satan's entrée into God's presence changes here. Now he really is kicked out of heaven, and he is furious. Note also that he carries with him the key to the bottomless pit.[120] He didn't have it before; it was given him by the One who holds the keys to heaven, hell and to death. To this point, all the destruction, havoc and misery that we have witnessed has been essentially man–made. God ordained it in heaven, but He allowed it to take place through natural means. Satan has to this point only used his ability as a liar

---

[118] Isaiah 14:12.

[119] Job 1:4.

[120] Revelation 9:1.

to deceive men and to use his trickery as the father of lies to counterfeit miracles. The destruction and havoc came about as a result of human ingenuity, so to speak. We invented the bombs that wipe a third of mankind from the face of the earth. All Satan did was convince us to use them.

SOMETHING NEW HAS BEEN ADDED

Now there is a new supernatural element added. Satan takes his new key and opens the bottomless pit to release the demons who were bound at the time of the great flood of Noah's day. They have such a vicious nature that GOD had to bind them to keep the human race from being annihilated before the appointed time—but now the restraints are off.

But GOD still does not permit even fallen man to be annihilated at this point. **"And out of the smoke came forth locusts upon the earth; and power was given them, as the scorpions of the earth have power. And they were told that they should not hurt the grass of the earth, nor any green thing, nor any tree, but only the men who do not have the seal of God on their foreheads. And they were not permitted to kill anyone, but to torment for five months; and their torment was like the torment of a scorpion when it stings a man."**[121]

GOD's instructions are in essence, "You may torment those who have the Antichrist's mark, but you may not kill them." Also, "you may not touch those who belong to Me." Satan's power is under strict control

---

[121] Revelation 9:3–5.

over those sealed by God—both now and in the Tribulation. Though this will be a period of great anguish, it is really the grace of GOD at work. I'm sure that the LORD is seeking to make mankind think because of this terrible torment and to decide to come to Him. It is written, "Men will seek death and will not find it; and they will long to die and death flees from them."

Sadly, most will choose death. As Billy Graham has often said, "The same sun that softens butter hardens clay."

CHAPTER 15

EAST ASSAULTS WEST

THE KINGS OF THE EAST

Following five months of torment by the demons

released from the bottomless pit, the first "woe"

is past. Men have suffered and cried out for death,

but it has eluded them. Mankind has had a tiny

respite from the battles of the War of Armageddon,

but now the second "woe" is unleashed.

> "And the sixth angel sounded, and I heard a
> voice from the four horns of the golden altar
> which is before God, one saying to the sixth
> angel who had the trumpet, 'Release the four
> angels who are bound at the great river
> Euphrates.' "[122]

God views the Euphrates River as the dividing line
between East and West. In fact, the old Roman
Empire also saw it that way. Everything east of the
Euphrates was called the Far East or Asia. The region
just to the west of the great river was known as the
Near East or Asia Minor.

ASIAN DEMONS OF DESTINY

According to the Bible, angels have always had a
tremendous influence on the affairs of men. To this
day, no successful mass invasion of the West has ever
been accomplished by an Eastern military force.
Every great conflict in which East meets West has
taken place east of the Euphrates River. The Bible
teaches that demons are territorial and have certain
assigned areas of authority within the satanically
controlled world system. That is, they influence the
human affairs of their respective areas.

The release of these four angels signals the lifting of
that Divine prohibition. The fact that they are called
the four angels indicates they are well–known and
that their role in history is well–known to GOD. They
were apparently bound thousands of years ago

[122] Revelation 9:13, 14.

because of their particularly vicious natures. The Bible reveals that some fallen angels are more malevolent than others are. And these four have apparently been reserved for this moment in history. When they are loosed, they immediately inspire the great population centers of Asia to launch an attack on the Western and Middle Eastern strongholds. These demons are effective, because they cause some one and a–half billion people, a third of the remaining population, to be killed in short order.

The Apostle John wrote, "**And the four angels, who had been prepared for the HOUR and DAY and MONTH and YEAR, were released, so** [for the purpose] **that they MIGHT KILL A THIRD OF MANKIND. And the number of the armies of the horsemen was TWO HUNDRED MILLION; I heard the number of them.**"[123]

SO MUCH FOR OVERPOPULATION!

I smile when I listen to the expositors of doom and gloom warning of a population explosion that threatens to destroy mankind. Sin threatens to destroy mankind, but overpopulation is hardly one of our long–term problems. In the Seal Judgments, one quarter of mankind dies at the hands of the rider on the pale horse. During the Trumpet Judgments, another third are destroyed in the various battles of the Armageddon War. When you add the two together, that represents a population reduction of

---

[123] Revelation 9:15, 16 NASB.

50%. As the Lord promised, if He failed to return on time, Earth's population would go from approximately six billion all the way down to zero.

THE ARMY OF 200 MILLION

John spoke of an army of 200 million men. The most reliable census figures of John's day would place the total population of the known world at about 500 million. In that context, the number he heard must have been incomprehensible to him. But it isn't incomprehensible to us. The Chinese army, including reserves and those of military age, is more than 300 million today! And the Bible doesn't restrict the invading army to just one country. We are in awe of the massive population of China, without really comprehending the vastness of the Indian population, which is within a fraction of being as great as that of China. China has just over a billion people. India has just under a billion people. Between these two nations alone reside nearly one third of the people living today.

By contrast, the United States, with all its territory, all its military and economic might, and all its prestige as the world's greatest super power, tips the scales at a mere 250 million. America could not field an army the size of John's vision if it conscripted everyone in the country between the ages of eight and 80, including the blind, crippled and crazy!

MORE NUKES

As in the Battle of Gog–Magog, nuclear weapons

seem to be indicated as a primary weapon of the army from the east. In John's vision, the invaders are a bizarre lot but they do have one theme that appears frequently in the Book of the Revelation.

> **"And this is how I saw in the vision the horses and those who sat on them: the riders had breastplates the color of fire and of hyacinth and of brimstone; and the heads of the horses are like the heads of lions; and out of their mouths proceed fire and smoke and brim-stone."**[124]

I believe that John is attempting to describe a mechanized army proceeding westward. The "riders" wear breastplates the color of fire and brimstone. We often refer to a brilliant red as "fiery." Brimstone is a yellowish color. The Chinese national flag is one large yellow star bordered by four smaller yellow stars against a field of fiery red! Since China is the largest (by far) of the eastern oriental nations, it is not too great a leap of logic to assume the Chinese battle standard would be emblazoned on the military vehicles. John tried to describe the "horses," since that is the only word he could use to describe a mechanized calvary. He said the heads of the horses are like the heads of lions. If you look at the turret of a Chinese tank, it does resemble a lion's head, at least in profile. And out of the "mouths" of these "horses" comes something I don't really think needs to be expounded on. Fire and brimstone. I think it obvious that John is viewing the use of both ICBM's and tactical battlefield nuclear

---

[124] Revelation 9:17.

weapons. A number of tactical nukes can be fired from a tank's main gun. Even *more* indicative of the power of these weapons is the body count.

> **"A third of mankind was killed by these three plagues, by the fire and the smoke and the brimstone, which proceeded out of their mouths."**[125]

In this one battle alone, a third of the remaining population of Planet Earth is ionized by a plague that combines three elements—fire, smoke and brimstone. Considering the fact that the human race has already been reduced by some 50% already, the population is dwindling fast. When the First Seal was opened, there were at least six billion people on earth, assuming the current population as a base. Reduce that by half, and we're looking at two and three–quarters billion people surviving the battle with the Kings of the East. When the smoke clears from that one, the population will be less than two billion people! And all of this horrible carnage, mind you, will happen within a time frame of less than two years. In fact, most of the terrible loss of life will occur with the lightning like suddenness of multiple missiles hitting targets of all sides in escalating waves of attacks.

For the sake of illustration, this would be fewer people than the current combined population of India and China. Another way of visualizing the dimension of this catastrophe would be like this: Suppose

---

[125] Revelation 9:18.

everyone on earth died except the Indians and Chinese. The rest of the entire world is wiped out, and they are the only ones left. That is the approximate mathematical equivalent to the population of the Tribulation who survive to this point.

The Prophet Isaiah predicted the terrible body count of this moment in history: **"Therefore, a curse devours the earth, and those who live in it are held guilty. Therefore, the inhabitants of the earth are burned, and few men are left"** (Isaiah 24:6). **"I will make mortal man scarcer than pure gold, and mankind than the gold of Ophir."**[126] And once again, The Lord Jesus Himself warned of this unparalleled tragedy, **"Unless those days are cut short, no one will be left alive...."**

A CAREFUL CHOICE OF WORDS

The Apostle John is staggered by the rebellion against God and the willingness of the survivors to continue in their immorality and idol worship. In his assessment of the worst of the litany of offenses against God, he lists those at the top of the hit parade.

> "And the rest of mankind, who were not killed by these plagues, did not repent of the works of their hands, so as not to worship demons, and the idols of gold and of silver and of brass and of stone and of wood, which can neither see nor hear nor walk; and they did not repent of their

---

[126] Isaiah 13:12.

murders nor of their sorceries nor of their immorality nor of their thefts."[127]

John is astonished to see that those not killed continue to turn to their pagan deities for relief instead of crying out to God. John's exasperation is evident, for he notes that their idols are impotent. They cannot see, hear or walk, yet mankind prefers to trust them for deliverance.

John chooses his words carefully when he describes the principal activities of the rebels as the Judgments continue to rain down upon the earth. He says they **"did not repent of their murders nor of their sorceries nor of their immorality nor of their thefts."**[128]

The word rendered "sorceries" occurs several times in Scripture. In the Old Testament it is translated from the Hebrew word *keseph,* which means "magic arts" or "witchcraft." In the New Testament, whenever "sorcery" or its derivatives appear, they come from the Greek root *magea,* which also means "magic arts."

But in the Book of the Revelation, "sorceries" is translated from *pharmakea,* φαρμακεα, which means, "the use or administration of drugs." Crimes like murder, prostitution and theft are standard operating procedure within the drug subculture. Isn't it interesting that the Holy Spirit inspired John to use that particular phrase here, in the passages that describe the conditions that define the sin–sick, drug–addled world in which we live today! To this generation, it makes perfect

---

[127] Revelation 9:20, 21.

[128] Revelation 9:21.

sense. In previous generations, the word association would not be quite so obvious. Remember, Daniel and John were both instructed to *"seal up"* or encode certain aspects of their visions **"until the time of the end, when knowledge would be increased."**[129] I don't think this was an offhand choice of words, but rather a clue left for this generation to help us recognize our place in the historical time line.

---

[129] Daniel 12:4.

CHAPTER 16

THE DEATH OF THE PRESENT WORLD ORDER

God's judgment of a lost and sinful world reaches

a fever pitch at this point. God has allowed the

policies of the Antichrist and his False Christ to

serve as the mechanism by which man's destruction

has been effected. Although each of the plagues

was conceived in heaven and delivered by an angel

opening a seal, or blowing a trumpet, that seal

or trumpet involved man–made machines of

destruction. God merely took the worst that man

had to offer and allowed him to run with it.

The unrestrained carnage of the first 14 Judgments proves to us, on this side of the Tribulation, just how effective the restraining influence of the Holy Spirit has been to this point. And it reveals the depths of God's love for us. Despite our rejection of Him and our outright hatred of Him throughout history, He proves Himself here by His absolute lack of restraint. As you read of the time of Jacob's Trouble that will come on the whole world, it's not too late to thumb over to the Book of Romans to see why you don't have to take part in this horrific nightmare period of future history.

> **"But God demonstrates His own love toward us, in that while we were yet sinners, Christ died for us. Much more then, having now been justified by His blood, we shall be saved from the wrath of God through Him."**[130]

THE GLOVES COME OFF

The **"wrath"** that those who are **"justified"** by His blood are saved from is described in the pages of this book. And from here on out, it is the wrath of God. Man has pretty much exhausted his arsenal. There are few popguns left, but not very much left to pop them. At least four billion people have perished in the first 14 Judgments alone. Now it's God's turn.

> **"And I heard a loud voice from the temple, saying to the seven angels, 'Go and pour out the seven bowls of the wrath of God into the earth.' "**[131]

---

[130] Romans 5:8, 9

[131] Revelation 16:1.

The first of these seven Bowls is a specific judgment against those who worshiped the dragon (Satan) which gave power to the beast by accepting his mark. Remember, the mark was necessary to conduct business during the Tribulation, but it was also a worship system. To accept it at all, is to accept it, Antichrist, false prophet and dragon, lock, stock and barrel. And God pours out on mankind His rage, accumulated over the course of human history.

THE FIRST BOWL—SKIN CANCER

> "And the first angel went and poured out his bowl into the earth; and it became a loathsome and malignant sore upon the men who had the mark of the beast and who worshiped his image."[132]

The Bowl Judgments have a historical precedent. At the Exodus, Pharaoh, a kind of antichrist, refused to surrender to the will of the One True God, preferring instead the signs and wonders offered by his court magicians. Egypt is often used as a metaphor in the Bible for the "world" as opposed to the Church. Note the similarity between the plagues here.

> "And it will become fine dust over all the land of Egypt, and will become boils breaking out with sores on man and beast through all the land of Egypt."[133]

---

[132] Revelation 16:2.

[133] Exodus 9:9.

THE SECOND BOWL—DEATH OF THE OCEANS

> "And the second angel poured out his bowl into the sea, and it became blood like that of a dead man; and every living thing in the sea died."[134]

There is a slight difference here between the judgment against Egypt and the judgment against mankind.

> "Thus says the Lord, 'By this you shall know that I am the Lord: behold, I will strike the water that is in the Nile with the staff that is in my hand, and it shall be turned to blood. And the fish that are in the Nile will die, and the Nile will become foul; and the Egyptians will find difficulty in drinking water from the Nile.' "[135]

In Egypt, the waters actually became blood. Even fresh water contained in jars became blood. It was a judgment, but one that was reversible. After Pharaoh repented, we can assume the water reverted back to water. There is no record of the entire Egyptian race perishing from thirst.

Then the LORD said to Moses: "Say to Aaron, 'Take your staff and stretch out your hand over the waters of Egypt, over their rivers, over their streams, and over their pools, and over all their reservoirs of water, that they may become blood; and there shall be blood throughout all the land of Egypt, both in vessels of wood and in vessels of stone.' "[136]

---

[134] Revelation 16:3.

[135] Exodus 7:17, 18.

[136] Exodus 7:19.

But God has prepared a permanent judgment against the waters of Planet Earth. Notice here that the water became like the blood of a dead man, and that every creature in the sea died. God has already prepared an organism that seems made to order for the job. We discussed that organism earlier in Chapter Eleven. I refer to the cell from hell, Pfeisteria. This is the strange new organism that caused the mysterious red tides first spotted off the coast of the Carolinas. This terrible organism literally boils fish alive by acting as a microscopic piranha. It has been dubbed the "Red Tide" or the "Cell from Hell." Both descriptions apply here.

THE THIRD BOWL— ALL FRESH WATER TURNED TO BLOOD

But man isn't going to get off any easier than Pharaoh did. The "red tide" is an irreversible ecological disaster designed to show God is not using any half measures. This is judgment, plain and simple. It is a permanent judgment. Only the Lord Jesus can and will reverse it. Just as Moses ordered even the drinking water turned to blood as a show of God's supernatural power, so too will the angel pollute the drinking water of man. And this time, John doesn't say it *looked* like blood. He said it *was*. This judgment was in return for the blood shed by those who refused to accept the Mark of the Beast and worship the dragon—and paid for it with their lives.

> "And the third angel poured out his bowl into
> the rivers and the springs of waters; and they
> became blood. And I heard the angel of the

**waters saying, 'Righteous art Thou, who art
and who wast, O Holy One, because Thou didst
judge these things; for they poured out the
blood of saints and prophets, and Thou hast
given them blood to drink. They deserve it.' "[137]**

For everyone who ever cried out to God for justice, for
everyone who ever thought that God didn't care, and
for everyone who ever thought someone wronged
them and got away with it, this verse is for you. God
keeps a tally book. He promises that vengeance
belongs to Him and that He will repay. He is making
reparations in the here and now for the crimes committed against His saints. Obviously, many of those
criminals are already dead. But death won't protect
them from the wrath of God...or the punishment
they have earned.

The punishment inflicted here is just an example of
what is awaiting the Hitlers, Stalins, Mao Tse Tungs
and Milosevics of this world, but also every guy who
ever persecuted a Christian or ever committed an
injustice against the innocent. At this point in history, God is making a point. If you haven't been
washed clean in the Blood of the Lamb, you will
assuredly drink of the blood of your victims. Sadly,
many people would just as soon take their chances.
I'm here to tell you, without the blood of Jesus Christ
to redeem you, you are reading your ultimate fate.
Once you find yourself on the other side of the
Church Age, if you embrace the system of Antichrist
and accept the mark, you have passed beyond hope.
This is your reality—now, and for eternity!

---

[137] Revelation 16:4–6.

THE FOURTH BOWL—
THE MOTHER OF ALL HEAT WAVES

At the time of this writing, a killer heat wave is raging across the eastern half of the globe. More than 3,000 people have died on the Indian continent following two months of daily temperatures as high as 120°F. A simultaneous heat wave in Egypt has already killed or hospitalized nearly 1,000 people. Hundreds have been hospitalized in Florida and across the Southwest. But that is nothing, compared to what this angel has to offer.

> **"The fourth angel poured out his bowl on the sun, and the sun was given power to scorch people with fire. They were seared by the intense heat and they cursed the name of God, who had control over these plagues, but they refused to repent and glorify him."**[138]

Can you imagine the Apostle John's astonishment as he witnesses these events? Despite all that he has seen, still he can't get over the fact that men reject the God who has the power over the plagues. Beyond that, they draw rasping, lung–searing heat into their lungs in order to gasp out blasphemies against the Name of God!

SUNBLOCK NO. 200 AIN'T STRONG ENOUGH

One of the most often repeated warnings heard in summer concerns the sun. "Be certain to wear sufficient

---

[138] Revelation 16:8, 9 NIV.

sunblock," you'll hear mothers warning children. Weather stations regularly give what is called "UV Ratings"—a measurement that tells how strong the sun's ultraviolet rays are. The ratings are based on the length of time it takes for the sun to damage uncovered skin. Without sufficient sunblock, overexposure of the skin to the sun results in melanoma. Melanoma is a painful, often fatal skin cancer that manifests itself in skin eruptions and open, oozing sores. One of the hallmarks of cancer is its propensity to spread over the affected area, growing worse and worse as it does so.

> "And the fifth angel poured out his bowl upon the throne of the beast; and his kingdom became darkened; and they gnawed their tongues because of pain, and they blasphemed the God of heaven because of their pains and their sores; and they did not repent of their deeds."[139]

ASIA'S ROUTE 66 WEST

This Sixth Bowl opens up the road to the final battles of the War of Armageddon. The Book of the Revelation is laid out in chronological order. But it also gives us the events from two perspectives, in order for us to be able to follow it with some measure of continuity. We see events from the heavenly perspective, and we see those same events from the earthly perspective. The Kings of the East are the monstrous army of 200 million whom we met in Chapter 15. They have now reached the western border.

---

[139] Revelation 16:10.

> "And the sixth angel poured out his bowl upon
> the great river, the Euphrates; and its water was
> dried up, that the way might be prepared for
> the kings from the east."[140]

The main force of the Kings of the East continues on
the march eastward, while the remaining armies of
the world all converge upon Israel. Satan is furious
that he hasn't been able to wipe out the only remaining trace of God on what he thinks is still his planet.
And, he still has just enough tricks up his sleeve to
convince the rest of the world that there's still a fighting chance against the God of all these plagues. You
might ask yourself, *just how gullible are these people,
anyway?* First, remember Satan has been given the
authority to work counterfeit miracles. Remember
also, **"all the nations were deceived by your** [his]
sorcery"[141] In the book that describes man's final
moments, twice does God reveal part of Satan's arsenal and call it by name. "Sorcery" or "Pharmakea"
or, the use of drugs. So this is a world stoned out of its
gourd. The worse things get, the more drugs they take
to make things bearable. To the drug–addled population of the planet, Satan presents the following:

> "And I saw coming out of the mouth of the
> dragon and out of the mouth of the beast and
> out of the mouth of the false prophet, three
> unclean spirits like frogs; for they are spirits of
> demons, performing signs, which go out to the
> kings of the whole world, to gather them

---

[140] Revelation 16:12.

[141] Revelation 18:22b.

together for the war of the great day of God, the Almighty."[142]

GATHER FOR WAR ?? ARE THEY NUTS?

In a word, yes! Driven mad by heat, drugs, water turning into blood, cancerous sores, grief and anger, the poor, demented remnant of the race of people who once proudly believed themselves to be the supreme beings of the universe gather together for one final battle.

"And they gathered them together to the place which in Hebrew is called Har–Magedon."[143]

"Har–Magedon" is, of course, the battlefield chosen for the final battle of the War of Armageddon. It is a broad plain near the ancient crossroads outpost city of Megiddo.

The War so far has not gone well for Antichrist and his armies. The final series of battles will take place at several locations.

---

[142] Revelation 16:13.

[143] Revelation 16:16.

CHAPTER 17

ARMAGEDDON'S FINAL BATTLES

THE BATTLE OF JEHOSHAPHAT

"For behold, in those days and at that time,

when I restore the fortunes of Judah and Jerusalem,

I will gather all the nations, and bring them down

to the valley of Jehoshaphat. Then I will enter into

judgment with them there on behalf of My people

and My inheritance, Israel, whom they have

scattered among the nations; and they have

divided up My land" (Joel 3:1, 2).

God dates this battle specifically. It takes place at the time when Israel has been restored to the land. The restoration of both the land and Jewish prosperity in it has never happened in any generation in history. This is the only one, and the only time. It cannot take place in some future time, following some future restoration.

This battle is a judgment in favor of Israel and a come uppance for those who have tried to divide up God's inheritance among those whose names weren't mentioned in the will.

The principals in this battle, I believe, will be the Israelis and the Palestinians who have attempted to usurp control over a city that holds no genuine significance for them and a land they never particularly wanted until the Jews occupied it again. God names the participants.

> "Moreover, what are you to Me, O Tyre, Sidon, and all the regions of Philistia? Are you rendering Me a recompense? But if you do recompense Me, swiftly and speedily I will return your recompense on your head."[144]

Tyre, Sidon and the regions of Philistia are the ancestral areas of the modern day Palestinians. God also takes exception to the argument that they claim the city in the name of God (Allah) and points out that they were never part of His sworn covenant that deeded it to the descendants of Abraham, Isaac and Jacob forever.

---

[144] Joel 3:4.

The Lord asks pointedly, **"Moreover, what are you to Me?"** The argument currently being put forth to justify Islam's claim to the city of Jerusalem is that it is a holy city and that Islam's aim in controlling the city is to ensure the "holy places" are respected. God hardly considers the claim. **"Are you rendering Me a recompense?"** God is plainly saying that He is quite capable of administering His city, thank you very much. He rejects the offer and hurls it back contemptuously.

God brings to mind the destruction of His Temple, and more specifically, the arrogance and hatred of those who usurped its grounds to build a monument to another deity. After the Temple was destroyed, the Romans scattered the Jews to the far corners of the earth. It was during this Diaspora that the city and the Temple Mount fell into the hands of Islam.

> **"You have taken My silver and My gold, brought My precious treasures to your temples, and sold the sons of Judah and Jerusalem to the Greeks in order to remove them far from their territory...."**[145]

God confirms that His prophecy to restore the Jews to the land of Promise has been fulfilled, and that it is from that place, the place He appointed for them, that He would gather them to battle and that they would be the instruments of his recompense—or, in common vernacular, *payback!*

---

[145] Joel 3:5, 6.

"Behold, I am going to arouse them from the place where you have sold them, and return your recompense on your head."[146]

WHEN JOHNNY COMES MARCHING HOME AGAIN

There was a popular song from the Civil War that began "When Johnny Comes Marching Home Again." Those who go up against the Israelis—and God Himself—might sing it on the way into the valley just east of Jerusalem. Nobody will be left to finish the last chorus, however.

The battle scene is horrific. The Antichrist gives the orders to his remaining generals, **"Proclaim this among the nations: Prepare a war; rouse the mighty men! Let all the soldiers draw near, let them come up! Beat your plowshares into swords, And your pruning hooks into spears."**[147]

A ROLL CALL FOR THE DAMNED

I always get a comical mental image when I read this next verse. In my mind's eye, I see this confused, cancer–ridden, dull–eyed, war–weary soldier. He smokes a giant joint and says, **"Let the weak say, 'I am a mighty man.'"**[148]

Notice, this is not the final battle of the War of Armageddon. The War of Armageddon involves the whole world in escalating waves of battles. But Joel

---

[146] Joel 3:1-7.

[147] Joel 3:10.

[148] Joel 3:10b.

sees those he can identify—the nations surrounding Israel. These are the same nations that are currently talking of peace and Oslo agreements, while preparing for war. War they want, and war they are certainly going to get.

> "Hasten and come, all you surrounding nations, and gather yourselves there. Bring down, O Lord, Thy mighty ones. Let the nations be aroused and come up to the valley of Jehoshaphat, for there I will sit to judge all the surrounding nations. Put in the sickle, for the harvest is ripe. Come, tread, for the winepress is full; the vats overflow, for their wickedness is great. Multitudes, multitudes in the valley of decision! For the day of the Lord is near in the valley of decision."[149]

Note again that the Battle of Jehoshaphat is *not* the final battle. It is a decisive battle, but not yet the final battle. Israel apparently releases more of its battlefield nuclear arsenal. Joel describes the hellish scene.

The Lord gives a gracious promise to sustain the believing remnant who are caught in the middle of the worst conflict of history:

> "The sun and moon grow dark, and the stars lose their brightness. And the Lord roars from Zion and utters His voice from Jerusalem, and the heavens and the earth tremble. But the Lord is a refuge for His people and a stronghold to the sons of Israel."[150]

---

[149] Joel 3:13.

[150] Joel 3:9–16.

Even in the midst of this horrible carnage, where all that is familiar is being destroyed, GOD assures the remnant that this will never happen again:

> "Then you will know that I am the Lord your God, Dwelling in Zion My holy mountain. So Jerusalem will be holy, and strangers will pass through it no more."[151]

---

[151] Joel 3:17.

CHAPTER 18

MANKIND'S ULTIMATE MADNESS

TIME FOR A SITUATION REPORT

I can only speculate on this situation,

using what is revealed by prophecy

with the latest intelligence on powers

that will be involved.

Each of the surviving powers in the final global conflict has land armies that have arrived in the area by this time. Most of the Russian and Muslim troops have been annihilated on the mountains of Israel.[152] There may still be a few elite divisions that made their way through to Jerusalem. Enough to wreak havoc around the city, but not enough to defeat the Roman–led Western armies.

Jerusalem was first besieged by an onslaught of the Russian–led Muslim alliance which included units from North and Black Africa. The Gog–Magog attack took the world leader by surprise, and it took him some time to muster the Western armies under his direct command for a counterattack.

> **"And at the end time the King of the South will collide with him, and the King of the North will storm against him with chariots, with horsemen, and with many ships; and he will enter countries, overflow them, and pass through."[153]**

The scene is devastating. Nuclear and neutron weapons have done serious damage to command and control, supply lines, lines of communication, and entire divisions no longer exist anywhere but on maps. In the confusion, the Bible seems to indicate Jerusalem is captured, recaptured, and captured again, but no one unit is able to hold it.

Evidently, either by treaty with the Jordanians, or by God's Providential protection of the Israelis who fled

---

[152] Ezekiel 39:2.

[153] Daniel 11:40.

to the caves at Petra,[154] Edom, Moab and the sons of Ammon (modern Jordan) are spared the wrath of the Antichrist's military forces.

Israel is only vulnerable to full–scale attack from two directions: from the north, and from the south. The mountains of Israel along the east form a natural barrier that make attack from that direction difficult, as the Russian/Muslim alliance is in the process of discovering.

By this time, the Antichrist has learned of the ICBM attacks launched by the invading Kings of the East. Remember, this is war, and things are happening quickly. Not all the details of the destruction of the Russian/Muslim army have fully reached him, and now he has to worry about 200 million Asian troops who have announced their intentions with mush-room clouds. He is furious and launches nuclear counterstrikes. An army of 200 million is pretty large, so his weapons are fairly effective. And the popula-tion continues to dwindle.

The battles grow so fierce, so destructive, and so wan-ton is the carnage that God sends Michael the archangel in on Israel's side. Remember, here we are in the midst of the greatest war in history, and Israel is right in the middle. Nuclear weapons, uncounted millions of invaders, the full force of the wrath of Satan is directed against the Jewish people.

"Now at that time Michael, the great prince who stands guard over the sons of your people,

---

> will arise. And there will be a time of distress
> such as never occurred since there was a nation
> until that time; and at that time your people,
> everyone who is found written in the book, will
> be rescued."[155]

Not every Jew will survive the war. God says that two thirds of the Jews will perish.

> "And it will come about in all the land," declares
> the Lord, "that two parts in it will be cut off and
> perish; but the third will be left in it. And I will
> bring the third part through the fire, refine them
> as silver is refined, and test them as gold is tested.
> They will call on My name, and I will answer
> them; I will say, 'They are My people,' and they
> will say, 'The LORD is my God.' "[156]

That remnant who are "refined as silver is refined" and "tested as gold is tested" will indeed call on the Lord. There is nothing more powerful than prayer.

> "But I will watch over the house of Judah, while
> I strike every horse of the peoples with blind-
> ness. Then the clans of Judah will say in their
> hearts, 'A strong support for us are the inhabi-
> tants of Jerusalem through the Lord of hosts,
> their God.' In that day I will make the clans of
> Judah like a firepot among pieces of wood and
> a flaming torch among sheaves, so they will
> consume on the right hand and on the left all
> the surrounding peoples, while the inhabitants

---

[155] Daniel 12:1.

[156] Zechariah 13:8, 9.

of Jerusalem again dwell on their own sites in Jerusalem."[157]

So, that is the military situation as it stands as the entire Middle East becomes the most heavily contested battlefield in human history.

THE BATTLE OF JERUSALEM

Once begun, the battles are fast and furious. As the Battle of Jehoshaphat draws to an ignominious end (for the Antichrist) the Battle of Jerusalem begins.

The war over the city of Jerusalem has been going on since the city was first sacked by Nebuchadnezzar in the 7th century before Christ, but, compared to the final battle, it was little more than a Cold War. According to the Prophet Zechariah, Jerusalem will be the focal point of the world's attention. That isn't too hard to imagine, given the current political climate. Scarcely a day passes without a headline story about Jerusalem—which is really fascinating, when you think about it. Just *why* should such a little city command such vast audiences? Particularly when you consider the fact that only a couple of generations ago, most people (in the developed world) thought Jerusalem was a mythical city, or a lost city from the Bible. Today it's the centerpiece of the world.

> "Behold, I am going to make Jerusalem a cup that causes reeling to all the peoples around; and when the siege is against Jerusalem, it will also be against Judah."[158]

---

[157] Zechariah 12:4b–6.

[158] Zechariah 12:2.

The grammatical construction of the word "against" used by Zechariah could also be rendered "because of" without changing the context or meaning. I believe that rendering is most appropriate here. All the remaining forces on earth could not be physically at, or even around, Jerusalem. The numbers are too vast, and the topography won't allow it. But, as we tour the future battlefields, we'll find each one has the capture of the city as part of its battle plan. Jerusalem was the issue over which the initial war was launched, which drags all other nations into it.

According to the ancient prophets, the battle for the city of Jerusalem will involve forces from every nation on the face of the earth. Once again, an interesting idea, originating as it does 2,500 years ago. The closest thing the world had ever seen to a global military force laying siege to any one city in history was during the Gulf War. Until the Gulf War, there was neither the political infrastructure nor the technical ability to fulfill such a prediction. If you were to ask a secular political analyst to guess what would be the target of any such multinational force in the future, odds are that he would predict Jerusalem. Of course, his guess would be based on his knowledge of the current world political situation. Zechariah had no other way of knowing, apart from Divine Revelation. But the context makes two things crystal clear. One is that the target will be Jerusalem. The other is that it involves a global, multinational military force.

> "And it will come about in that day that I will make Jerusalem a heavy stone for all the peoples;

all who lift it will be severely injured. And all
the nations of the earth will be gathered
against it."[159]

It is during the battle for Jerusalem that the national
redemption of Israel is accomplished. Every promise
of God is true, and the covenant God made with
Abraham is redeemed. The absolute Biblical proof
that destroys the argument of the Dominionists and
the Kingdom Now Movement is declared in no
uncertain terms.

"And it will come about in that day," declares
the Lord of hosts, "that I will cut off the names
of the idols from the land, and they will no
longer be remembered; and I will also remove
the prophets and the unclean spirit from the
land."[160]

There will be no atheists left among the children of
Abraham in that day. The Antichrist's claims to
Messiahship will be forever and unconditionally dis-
credited, and Israel will see, recognize and mourn the
Son that their fathers in their blindness, "cut off
from the earth."[161]

"And I will pour out on the house of David and
on the inhabitants of Jerusalem, the Spirit of
grace and of supplication, so that they will look
on Me whom they have pierced; and they will
mourn for Him, as one mourns for an only son,

---

[159] Zechariah 12:3.

[160] Zechariah 13:2.

[161] Daniel 9:26.

and they will weep bitterly over Him, like the bitter weeping over a first–born."[162]

THE INCREDIBLE MELTING ARMY

As the battle rages, the Jews are spiritually energized. The recognition of their Messiah gives them supernatural fighting ability. At last they can be certain that they are in one accord with the God of Abraham, Isaac and Jacob, as they were in the days of Joshua. The invaders unleash their ultimate weapon at this point. Satan knows the true nature of Jerusalem, that it is the City of God. He doesn't want to destroy the city; he wants to possess it. From the beginning, that was his plan.

> "But you said in your heart, 'I will ascend to heaven; I will raise my throne above the stars of God, and I will sit on the mount of assembly in the recesses of the north. I will ascend above the heights of the clouds; I will make myself like the Most High.' "[163]

The "mount of assembly" is the Temple Mount. Satan wants to possess it so badly that the first order of business for his False Messiah was to order the building of the Third Temple. Once that was accomplished, "he took his seat on the mercy seat in the holy of holies and proclaimed himself to be God."[164]

---

[162] Zechariah 12:10.

[163] Isaiah 14:13, 14.

[164] 2 Thessalonians 2:4.

So Satan's Antichrist isn't about to allow nukes to destroy his chosen capital. Neither will Satan. But he does have a weapon in his arsenal that he can use to wipe out God's people without destroying his coveted "mount of assembly." It is at this point that he unleashes the weapon that he knows the Jews hate the most. The plan is more than just to kill the Jews, it is to destroy them in the most abominable way possible. It was the Jews God chose to reveal Himself to the nations through. It was the Jews who recorded the true nature of Satan as a liar. Satan's ultimate Enemy, Jesus Christ, the Son of God, was a Jew. Satan hates the Jews above all humanity. During the Holocaust, he inspired Hitler's henchmen with a new, terrifying weapon that left an indelible imprint on the Jewish consciousness. He unleashes it now, in the hope of breaking their spirit as he takes their lives. Gas.

During most of the 1990s, chemical weapons production plants in Aleppo and Damascus, together with a huge facility in Libya, have been operating round the clock, stockpiling VX gas and other chemical and biological weapons for just the right moment. This is a pretty terrible weapon. But it is also imprecise. All that is necessary is for the wind to shift.

> "In that day," declares the Lord, "I will strike every horse with bewilderment, and his rider with madness. But I will watch over the house of Judah, while I strike every horse of the peoples with blindness."[165]

---

[165] Zechariah 12:4.

The Israelis respond using their own terror weapon—the battlefield neutron bomb. It unleashes a burst of radiation so intense that it literally vaporizes all living things within its kill zone—without damaging buildings or structures. And the radiation dissipates quickly, leaving the battlefield radiation levels within safe limits almost immediately. The Israelis also want to preserve the "mount of the congregation"—but for its Rightful Heir. Zechariah characterizes the use of these weapons as a "plague" but describes them in terms that fit perfectly with the use of neutron bombs.

> **"Now this will be the plague with which the Lord will strike all the peoples who have gone to war against Jerusalem; their flesh will rot while they stand on their feet, and their eyes will rot in their sockets, and their tongue will rot in their mouth."**[166]

THE BATTLE OF THE JORDAN VALLEY

As the battles rage in Jerusalem and the Valley of Jehoshaphat, what is left of the divisions of the northern army defeated on the mountains of Israel withdraw to regroup. They head down the Jordan Valley near the Dead Sea.

> **"But I will remove the northern army far from you, and I will drive it into a parched and desolate land, and its vanguard into the eastern sea."**[167]

---

[166] Zechariah 14:12.

[167] Joel 2:20.

The Jordan Valley runs some 200 miles from the North Sea of Galilee to Eilat. Into this valley streams the remaining hordes from the East, to meet in battle with what remains of both the Russian/Muslim alliance and the armies of the Antichrist.

WHY THE KINGS OF THE EAST?

We can discern from the Bible four distinct spheres of power in the last days. The northern power (Russia), the Kings of the East (the Asian power), the Revived Roman Empire (Antichrist), and the pan–Arab power (Kings of the South). Early in the Tribulation, all were more or less allied with the Antichrist. Revelation 13 says that without being part of the Antichrist's system, no man could buy or sell. But something happens to break up that alliance. The Bible says that the Russians are motivated by an "evil thought." Most likely, it is jealousy that Europe is getting all the attention. The Kings of the East want their share of the pie as well, and they don't think they're getting it. Admittedly, this is speculation, but that is also the historical reason behind the current political standoff between the West and Russia, and between Red China and the rest of the world. Everybody wants to be the number–one super power. In the Battle of the Jordan Valley, the collected armies of the world meet to settle that issue against the backdrop of the ongoing battles elsewhere in the Middle East.

THE LAST GREAT CONFLICT

This is the "valley of decision" spoken of by the

Prophet Joel.[168] All the nations of the world will be represented at this "mother of all battles." When Saddam Hussein used the term to describe his fantasy of the ground war between his forces and the coalition, I had to smile. Even in his wildest fantasy, Saddam couldn't picture anything like this! The Jordan Valley will one day contain an army numbering in the hundreds of millions of men. Plus equipment, weapons, artillery pieces, vehicles, the works! Just imagine the dust such an assemblage will kick up!

Keep in mind that this last, greatest battle is part of a lightning war. Some of the battle scenes I've described here occur virtually simultaneously. For that reason, there are elements in each battle scene—like the Russian/Muslim alliance, that play key roles throughout. The overall end of the Gog–Magog alliance is annihilation, but yet they can be found in each scenario.

GOG'S BATTLE PLAN

The Russians will launch their attack on Israel at the same time as the Kings of the South (the pan–Arab confederation) make their push. The Russians will capture key ports, like the one at Haifa—that will lead directly into the valley of decision, arriving from the west.

Meanwhile, the Kings of the East (the Red Chinese alliance) are arriving from the east into this same

---

[168] Joel 3:14.

valley. The Kings of the South are already there. And the Antichrist and his forces, including the whole of the Western world (sadly, that will include America) will be on the march to repel the invaders.

This happens on the heels of multiple nuclear attacks, chemical and biological warfare, and the almost certain loss of sophisticated communications technology like satellites, global positioning systems, television and telephones, *etc.* Nobody really knows what they are up against until they square off!

SURPRISES ALL AROUND

Undoubtedly, each believes that he is leading an over-whelming force against an enemy in disarray. The Antichrist's forces are simply repelling an Arab inva-sion and retaliating against a nuclear attack. The Kings of the East are planning to take the Middle East and its oil for themselves. With 200 million men, they certainly believe they have the advantage. Russia thinks it has the advantage of surprise. And suddenly, there they are! The whole world in a single, massive confrontation. Awesome! Picture the scene as the prophet Joel saw it.

> "A day of darkness and gloom, a day of clouds and thick darkness. As the dawn is spread over the mountains, so there is a great and mighty people; there has never been anything like it, nor will there be again after it to the years of many generations."[169]

[169] Joel 2:2.

Joel captures, through the inspiration of the Holy Spirit, the madness, the hopelessness, and the insanity of the moment. Ordinary soldiers, led by demoniacs who have assured them of victory, looking back toward home and country, now under the shadow of the mushroom cloud. And in front, more war, more devastation.

> **"A fire consumes before them, and behind them a flame burns."**[170]

The common perception of the armies assembled at Armageddon is somehow unhuman, ethereal. But the participants are men, with wives and children. Men who had mortgages to pay, and jobs to work at. These are not satanic robots in the classical sense. They are no different from the soldiers of any contemporary army. They are just following their leaders. Except now, that is all they have. Nuclear war has robbed them of everything else. Their only hope for a continued existence is to find someplace untouched by the devastation. Like Israel.

> **"The land is like the garden of Eden before them, but a desolate wilderness behind them, and nothing at all escapes them."**[171]

---

[170] Joel 2:3a.

[171] Joel 2:3b.

CHAPTER 19

JUST IN TIME

SO, WHO WON?

The assembled armies of Planet Earth are

engaged in combat. So many have died that

the valley is neck–deep in blood. Millions and

millions of soldiers have died in this one valley,

during this one engagement. The scene defies

description; but John, under the inspiration of

the Holy Spirit, captures the moment.

"And the angel swung his sickle to the earth, and
gathered the clusters from the vine of the earth,
and threw them into the great wine press of the
wrath of God. And the wine press was trodden
outside the city, and blood came out from the
wine press, up to the horses' bridles, for a distance of two hundred miles."[172]

There is only one valley in Israel that fits the mile
description. It is the Jordan Valley, which extends
from just north of the Sea of Galilee to Eilat at the
Red Sea. Because of the intense radiation, blood will
not coagulate. It will literally become a sea of blood
five feet deep.

A WORLD GONE MAD

While the battle rages in the Jordan Valley, the Battle
of Jerusalem is in full swing. Virtually the entire
globe is locked in combat. The planet is rocked and
shaken by multiple nuclear detonations. It seems as
if the world has gone mad. Insanity reigns supreme.
Compassion and mercy are nonexistent. Every man's
hand is turned against his brother. Anyone who has
ever been in combat has some idea of just how cruel
war can be.

A LIVING NIGHTMARE

Picture, if you can, the scenes at the Nazi death
camps during World War II. Guards herding women
and children naked into the showers. Attack dogs

---

[172] Revelation 14:19, 20.

mauling fleeing victims. The smoke of the crematori-
ums rising into the sky. Add to that the images of
mushroom clouds. Imagine the whole world through
the lenses of the combat cameras that captured the
scenes during the Normandy invasion. Roll it all
together with the worst nightmare you ever had.
Armageddon!

> **"And I will shew wonders in the heavens and in
> the earth, blood, and fire, and pillars of
> smoke."**[173]

Suddenly, a Light more intense, more brilliant than
the flash of an atomic bomb cuts across the sky, shin-
ing from east to west.

> **"And I saw heaven opened; and behold, a white
> horse, and He who sat upon it is called Faithful
> and True; and in righteousness He judges and
> wages war. And His eyes are a flame of fire, and
> upon His head are many diadems; and He has
> a name written upon Him which no one knows
> except Himself. And He is clothed with a robe
> dipped in blood; and His name is called The
> Word of God. And the armies which are in
> heaven, clothed in fine linen, white and clean,
> were following Him on white horses. And from
> His mouth comes a sharp sword, so that with it
> He may smite the nations; and He will rule
> them with a rod of iron; and He treads the wine
> press of the fierce wrath of God, the Almighty.
> And on His robe and on His thigh He has a**

---

[173] Joel 2:30 KJV.

name written, 'KING OF KINGS, AND LORD OF LORDS.' "[174]

The Antichrist orders his troops to stop fighting and turn their weapons toward this new Warrior and His army. The Asian commanders do the same thing. Incredibly, they comply. This action, in and of itself, demonstrates the madness of the moment!

> "And I saw the beast and the kings of the earth and their armies, assembled to make war against Him who sat upon the horse, and against His army."[175]

The Lord puts His foot down on the Mount of Olives. It splits in two, creating a chasm into which the believers can seek refuge until the awful carnage is completed. It's interesting to note that there is a fault line that runs under the Mount of Olives that moves in exactly the same direction that the Bible prophesies.

> "Then the Lord will go forth and fight against those nations, as when He fights on a day of battle. And in that day His feet will stand on the Mount of Olives, which is in front of Jerusalem on the east; and the Mount of Olives will be split in its middle from east to west by a very large valley, so that half of the mountain will move toward the north and the other half toward the south. And you will flee by the valley of My mountains, for the valley of the mountains will

---

[174] Revelation 19:11–16.

[175] Revelation 19:19.

reach to Azel; yes, you will flee just as you fled
before the earthquake in the days of Uzziah
king of Judah."[176]

Then it's over. The Warrior, Jesus Christ, has returned
as He promised, before mankind could destroy itself,
along with the believers that the Lord promised
would be protected until He comes. The carnage is
incredible. Those not already killed during the battles
are slain by the Word of God.

"And I saw an angel standing in the sun; and
he cried out with a loud voice, saying to all the
birds which fly in midheaven, "Come, assemble
for the great supper of God; in order that you
may eat the flesh of kings and the flesh of commanders and the flesh of mighty men and the
flesh of horses and of those who sit on them and
the flesh of all men, both free men and slaves,
and small and great."[177]

THE CHRONOLOGY OF JUDGMENT

As I said earlier, the Book of the Revelation is laid
out in chronological order. Because so many events
occur simultaneously, oftentimes students of Bible
prophecy tend to organize them in a linear fashion.
In so doing, it is easy to get events out of sequence.
The whole purpose of this book is to document the
sequence of events that make up the War of
Armageddon and the return of Jesus Christ. The

---

[176] Zechariah 14:3–5.

[177] Revelation 19:17, 18.

battles occur in a specific order, and are outlined from two perspectives—the view from heaven and the view from earth. Some of what John saw was revealed to him when he was called into heaven in Revelation Chapter 4. The remainder of John's record was compiled from his observations from his vantage point of being an observer of future earthly events. John saw both the cause and effect, although both perspectives record the same developments.

Each of the Judgments is in order. Like the birth pangs that Jesus used as an analogy, they grow closer together and more intense with each subsequent judgment. The First Seal, the rise of the Antichrist, takes three and a-half years. The Gog–Magog War, the opening shot in the War of Armageddon, could take a year or more to play out. Here is an outline view, in order, of the battle plan of the greatest war of all time:

- Antichrist takes his seat in the Temple—Israel recognizes that they've been conned. He's not God.

- Believing Israelis flee to the mountains of Jordan (expected to be Petra) where they will be Divinely protected. (Matthew 24:15–22; Revelation 12:6, 13–17).

- The Antichrist sets up his 666 economic system and begins an all–out campaign of persecution against the Tribulation saints.

- The Russian/Muslim alliance (Gog–Magog) begin their campaign against Israel. In a two–pronged attack, the alliance sweeps into Israel while simultaneously moving south into Africa. The West responds using nuclear weapons.

- As a consequence of the Gog–Magog invasion, the world polarizes into four identifiable spheres of power. The Muslim alliance with Russia isolates the East. Thermonuclear attacks isolate the Antichrist's western powerbase. The Russian attack on Africa galvanizes a pan–African alliance.

- Israel apparently uses both thermonuclear and neutron devices against Egypt, Russia, Iran, Iraq and Syria (Ezekiel 39:6).

- The Eastern forces destroy that part of the alliance that is on the mountains of Israel (Ezekiel 38:22, 23; Daniel 11:40–45; Joel 2:20, 21).

- The ecological damage caused by that war, together with the collateral damage done by the nuclear exchanges, causes economic chaos, food shortages, famine, plagues—and the war escalates. This is reflected in the Third and Fourth Seal Judgments. All this is a consequence of the war between the West and the Russian/Muslim alliance.

- A third of all ships, submarines and sea life is destroyed.

- A third of all fresh water is poisoned

- A quarter of the earth's population is killed.

- The Kings of the East begin to mobilize a 200 million man army. To cover that mobilization, they launch a nuclear attack against the West. By this time, more than half of mankind has perished.

- Nuclear radiation and debris = nuclear winter.

- A third of the celestial light (sun, moon, stars) is blocked out because of the debris from explosions and fires (Isaiah 13:9, 10, 23, 24).
- Satan is expelled from heaven.
- He releases vicious demons out of the bottomless pit.
- The Asian army collides with the Antichrist–led Western army
- The War of Armageddon begins.
- The Battle of Jehoshaphat takes place in a valley east of Jerusalem (Joel 3:1, 2, 9–15).
- The Battle of Jerusalem (Zechariah 12:2, 3; 14:1–14; Revelation 14:20; Daniel 11:45).
- The Battle of Jordan Valley/Dead Sea (Joel 2:20; Revelation 14:20).
- The Battle of the Mountains of Moab, Edom, Bozrah (Isaiah 34:5–9; 6:3).
- Christ destroys the armies seeking to kill the Divinely protected believers, as the first order of business on His return.
- The Battle of Meggido/Jezreel—what is called the Battle of Armageddon, or Har–Megiddo (Revelation 16:16).
- An all–out global battle takes place (Isaiah 24:1–23; Zephaniah 1:14–18; Ezekiel 39:6; Isaiah 34:1–17).
- Jesus sets His foot down on the Mount of Olives.
- He destroys all the armies that are fighting against Jerusalem (Zechariah 14:12).

- He "resets" the planet's ecology, which is no longer viable to sustain life.
- He gathers all surviving Jews to judge at Sinai (Ezekiel 20:33–44; Zephaniah 3:8–13; 13:8, 9).
- He gathers all gentile survivors to judge at Jehoshaphat Valley (Matthew 25:31).

PERFECTION, AT LAST, FOR A WHILE

Once Jesus has cleaned up our mess, He takes over His rightful place as the Judge and the head of human government. What a different world it is! The world is restored to its original state, the curse against the planet is lifted. Human life spans are restored to what they were prior to the Flood.

Isaiah, speaking under the inspiration of the Holy Spirit, paints a beautiful word picture of a world that we poor mortals can only dream of:

> **"No longer will there be in it an infant who lives but a few days, or an old man who does not live out his days; for the youth will die at the age of one hundred and the one who does not reach the age of one hundred shall be thought accursed."**[178]

The Fall of man in the Garden of Eden occurred as the result of two things. The first was the deception that man could be like God. That was what tripped Satan up, remember? He used that same defect to trip up humanity. The second was pride. God allowed both Satan and humanity to have their chance at

---

[178] Isaiah 65:20.

playing God. We have just spent an entire book discussing how well that worked.

You'd think we finally learned our lesson, wouldn't you? You'd be wrong. For 1,000 years man will live in harmony with the Creator, Jesus Christ. During that time, life on earth will be relatively the same as it is now, but without the bad stuff. People will be born during the Millennium and live their entire lives under the government of Jesus Christ. Faith won't be the issue; they'll know Him like we know our president. The question of whether or not God exists will never come up. If somebody wants to know, they can go to Jerusalem and ask Him.

At the end of the 1,000 years, Satan is released for a short time from his prison and allowed to deceive the world again. Believe it or not, he's successful.

A WORD TO THE WISE

One of the greatest lessons we can learn from God's plan of the ages is that He starts man's history with a perfect environment, and He ends it with a perfect environment. In both cases, the reality of God is not in question and communication with God is possible. Yet in both situations, man makes a free choice to reject God and believe Satan's lie about Him.

This is a frightening commentary on man's basic nature. Our most basic need is not to improve our environment, education, economic status, or even to have infallible evidence that God exists and is knowable.

Jesus gave the only answer for mankind long ago in simple terms, **"I tell you the truth, no one can see** [understand] the kingdom of God unless he is born again [Greek, "from above"].... **Flesh gives birth to flesh, but the Spirit gives birth to spirit"** (John 3:3, 6).

You see, we are all born physically alive, but spiritually dead. Man died spiritually at the moment of the first rebellion against God. From that time forward, every human being was born without the spiritual life that originally enabled him to know God on a personal level. To know God, we must have the same kind of life He does.

In our natural state, we can't be sure that God is there. Through our physical intelligence, we can see evidences of His existence all about us. But we cannot know Him personally until we have reborn within us a spiritual nature. It is almost impossible to explain a sunset to a man born blind. But if you could suddenly give him sight, the problem is resolved immediately. He doesn't need any further scientific evidences about the properties of light and color, *et al.*

The one great obstacle to man receiving this spiritual birth was his sinful nature with which he was born. For this reason, God stepped out of eternity into time and became one of us, only without the effects of sin. He lived a perfect life of obedience on our behalf in order to qualify to bear our judgment. On the cross, He was judged for every sin that you or I will ever commit. By this great act, motivated by His love, He purchased a pardon for all mankind.

There is a pardon with your name on it, reserved in heaven. But it will only become valid when you personally admit your need and receive it. Right now, tell Jesus that you receive your gift of pardon. Invite Him to come into your life and make it pleasing to God.

I'm going to assume that you just prayed that prayer. So I will see you at His feet when the trumpet calls.

Maranatha!

WESTERN FRONT
P U B L I S H I N G

Also By Hal Lindsey

APOCALYPSE CODE

In this riveting nonfiction book the father of modern-day prophecy cracks the "Apocalypse Code" and deciphers long-hidden messages about man's future and the fate of the Earth. **ISBN 1-888848-21-9**

BLOOD MOON

Hal Lindsey's ONLY Novel! From the desert tents of Abraham to the year 2014. What happens in-between defies imagination.
ISBN 1-888848-07-3

PLANET EARTH 2000 AD

Berserk global weather, the crime explosion, an emerging New World Order...What does it all mean? Once again, no one puts it all in perspective like Hal Lindsey in this exciting and revealing report on the dangers facing the world at the end of the 20th century. **ISBN 1-888848-05-7**

AMAZING GRACE

This book recounts the personal experience of "Amazing Grace" in Hal Lindsey's own life. It reveals, in a clear and easy-to-understand manner the Biblical basis of why AMAZING GRACE is the only answer to mankind's need for meaning, purpose and fellowship with God.
ISBN 0-9641058-4-5

THE FINAL BATTLE

Want to know what hell on earth will be like? Hal Lindsey gives us the best glimpse to date. This book is sure to shock as many people to God as did THE LATE GREAT PLANET EARTH. **ISBN 0-9641058-2-9**

For a Complimentary Catalog

of Hal Lindsey's Books, Audio Tapes & Videos, *please call*

To Book HAL LINDSEY for Speaking Engagements

or

To Hear MORE INFORMATION About

- Upcoming Conferences
- Newsletter Subscriptions
- Tours to the Holy Land
- Release Dates for New Books & Videos

please contact

WESTERN FRONT LTD

800-764-0012

WESTERN FRONT
PUBLISHING